"Once-in-a-generation leader Mike Signorelli and his catalyst of clarion warriors deliver a treasure trove of tactical insights marshaled to empower and sustain lasting revival! *Fire Starters* pulls no punches as each tenured voice unleashes revelation power destined to advance revival in your own life. Prepare to be spiritually weaponized for kingdom longevity!"

Joseph Z, author, broadcaster, prophetic voice, JosephZ.com

"I have profound respect for Mike Signorelli for many reasons, but I must say the term *fire starter* is perhaps the greatest description I've heard to describe him. He, his wife, and their ministry have been used by God to light powerful spiritual fires that have driven back darkness and set people ablaze for Jesus by the power of the Holy Spirit. If anyone is qualified to skillfully compile the material you are about to read in this book, it is Mike. I urge you to read it, as I have done, from beginning to end—and to ask God to make you a fire starter for this generation!"

Rick Renner, minister, author, broadcaster, Moscow, Russia

"The spirit of revival is more easily caught than taught. To become a true fire starter, you need impartation more than information because it requires a transfer of spiritual DNA. In a world desperate for something real, this book will serve as a spark in hungry hearts. Mike Signorelli has gathered voices who don't just talk revival . . . they breathe it. Like firebrands tied to foxes' tails, these words will ignite wherever they land. If you've ever cried out, 'Where are the Elijahs of our day?' look no further. They are here, and they are passing you the torch. Read it. Carry it. Burn with it."

Alan DiDio, host of *Encounter Today*, pastor of
The Encounter Charlotte

FIRE STARTERS

BOOKS BY MIKE SIGNORELLI

Inherit Your Freedom

Fire Starters

FIRE STARTERS

**Igniting Revivals
and Sustaining
Spiritual
Awakening**

MIKE SIGNORELLI
Compiler

Chosen
a division of Baker Publishing Group
Minneapolis, Minnesota

Published by Chosen Books
Minneapolis, Minnesota
ChosenBooks.com

Chosen Books is a division of
Baker Publishing Group, Grand Rapids, Michigan

Library of Congress Cataloging-in-Publication Data
Names: Signorelli, Mike editor
Title: Fire starters : igniting revivals and sustaining spiritual awakening / Mike Signorelli, compiler.
Other titles: Fire starters (Baker Publishing Group)
Description: Minneapolis, Minnesota : Chosen, a division of Baker Publishing Group, [2025] | Includes bibliographical references.
Identifiers: LCCN 2025002671 | ISBN 9780800773151 (paperback) | ISBN 9780800773229 (casebound) | ISBN 9781493450534 (ebook)
Subjects: LCSH: Evangelistic work
Classification: LCC BV3790 .F5417 2025 | DDC 269/.2—dc23/eng/20250416
LC record available at https://lccn.loc.gov/2025002671

Cover design by Humble Books (HumbleBooksMedia.com)

Baker Publishing Group publications use paper produced from sustainable forestry practices and postconsumer waste whenever possible.

25   26   27   28   29   30   31   7   6   5   4   3   2   1

I dedicate this book to every ember that,
despite the harshest conditions,
refuses to fade without becoming a flame.
—Mike Signorelli

CONTENTS

FOREWORD

LOU ENGLE

In what looked like a broken-down inner city neighborhood, I was led into a dark, nondescript building. Stepping inside, I saw what was anything but nondescript. I was plunged into a fire pit of spiritual passion, explosive and joyful worship, transformed lives, testimonies of deliverance from witchcraft and sexual addictions so dynamic I was taken back. Then this man, Mike Signorelli, whom I had met before but knew nothing of his ministry, began to speak of this love invasion of darkness, church planting, hell invading movement. I thought, "Who is this guy?" He's a burning, shining lamp, a new breed of apostle, a fire starter, and a fire sustainer.

There are others, you know. Many others! Raised up by God's passion for the world and arising out of this "death of civilization" collapsing culture, these consecrated and anointed ones, forged out of the fires of fasting and prayer, persevering through the deserts of divine dealings and delays and then lifted into God-given prophetic encounters and dreams of destiny, risk all to follow Jesus and frame the future with Him. They are prophets who see and proclaim an alternate reality to the present entrapment under a universal lie. They are "to the winner take all" evangelists who break through governmental and demonic obstacles to win masses for Christ. They are the ones who carry bags of seeds of spiritual hunger and throw them everywhere, lifting up lovers and worshipers of God in a generation starved for the Presence. They are the burning ones who live and build for *revival*, and all who gather around them light their candles to their torch. They are normal people like you and me who believe in a great God and that He can live great in them. Finally, they are great leaders who give articulation to that which is being groaned in the masses, thus causing bones to rattle and movements to occur that destroy false ideologies and structures of oppression, bring healing to families, reform cities and nations, and bring the longed-for future into the present, the Kingdom of God.

Now in his new book, *Fire Starters*, Signorelli gathers an amazing company of this new breed of movement makers and torchbearers to tell their stories, teach their ways and wisdom, and inspire and inflame all those who read to run and blaze across the earth.

Oh, that thousands will read this burning book, draw near to its flame, and hear their names being called, and then go forth with their little rod and the great I AM to light fires all over the world.

Lou Engle
President of Lou Engle Ministries

INTRODUCTION

MIKE SIGNORELLI

For generations, many of God's greatest leaders have departed this world with the baton still clutched in their hands, unable or unwilling to pass on their unique lessons—be those failures or successes. What if there existed a book that could serve as that baton? Imagine the possibility of being mentored by leading revivalists and movement makers from previous eras, engaging in conversations about their personal failures and public triumphs. Picture yourself pulling up a seat, as if they were speaking directly to you, receiving wisdom that cost them entire seasons of their lives. While we have access to sermons and private journals from the spiritual giants of old, there hasn't been a comparable level of intentionality in transmitting their knowledge, until now.

Fire Starters—those anointed individuals who could discern how to transform desperate and dry conditions into smoldering embers—have revolutionized our perspectives, methodologies, and perceptions in both culture and the expression of the kingdom of heaven on earth. They possessed the ability to nurture embers and fan smoldering circumstances into flames of revival. These visionaries knew how to kindle seemingly insignificant sparks until they blazed into full-fledged movements. But what happens when the art of making fire isn't transmitted to the next generation? What are the consequences when only fragmented and isolated strategies are passed on? We find ourselves doomed to learn the hard way, "pioneering" when we should be inheriting!

As I write this, the world is undergoing a great transition. My international travels over the past several years have revealed the formation of a global monoculture, facilitated by the internet and the widespread exchange of information. Demonic agendas that threaten the existence of the traditional family are influencing governments and infiltrating educational systems. An entire generation is slipping into despair as moral decay and relativism grip the minds of the masses. Suicide rates are increasing, while fertility rates decline. Under the guise of "freedom," we are being told that we can choose our own fate, apart from the "delusion of God." Yet in the midst of this confusion and uncertainty, a special hunger is rising. Despite the narratives and propagation of human agendas, a remnant is yearning for God. In defiance of being told that we are gods ourselves, that God doesn't exist, or that nature is God, many are turning to Jesus Christ—the only true and living God.

Fire Starters don't curse dry ground; they strike it and create a spark! They don't merely diagnose the environment and complain; they assess and execute until the change becomes a reality. What feels like uncertainty to the world is identified as opportunity by a Fire Starter. What appears impossible to the world is recognized as God's divine opportunity by these burning ones.

There are many in my generation who share this calling to be Fire Starters. I'm privileged to pursue this high calling alongside them. God assembles teams with each member carrying a revelation of heaven's DNA and expressing an aspect of Christ's ministry on earth through the Holy Spirit. While the finite pages of this book couldn't possibly contain the totality of what there is to learn from this generation, I believe the Holy Spirit has highlighted what needs to be passed on as an inheritance to you. As you read this, know that we are counting on you. Heaven is counting on you. Your "yes," lockstep with Jesus Christ, is all that is needed to fan the flames.

This book serves as a bridge between generations, a conduit for the wisdom of the past to reignite the fires of the future. It is an invitation to join the ranks of Fire Starters, to learn from their triumphs and tribulations, and to carry the flame of revival into a world desperate for divine intervention. As you turn these pages, may you not only receive the baton, but may you also be empowered to run your leg of this spiritual relay with passion and purpose.

I want to encourage you as you journey through these pages. I believe that learning from the Fire Starters in this book will be one of the most clarifying experiences concerning your role in the Body of Christ and your position in history. We are examining the past in order to empower you to create the future. Reading this book will be one of the single greatest investments that you can make in yourself. Most of us come from very humble beginnings. I was born to a single mother and raised in a tin trailer outside of Chicago. I'm the eldest of five children, all fatherless. I became the first-generation full-time minister in my family, but if you asked those who knew me, they would tell you I was the least likely. Severely incapable, yet completely empowered by the Holy Spirit after a fateful event in my bedroom at fifteen years old—I serve as a witness that with God, all things are possible. When you're in the company of revivalists, your dreams and visions are never intimidating. A company of generals will spur you on for more. That's why we put this book together. It's really not about us; it's about what's possible through you when you say "yes," completely.

A fellow Fire Starter,

Mike Signorelli

1

CONSECRATION AND REVIVAL

JEREMIAH JOHNSON

God is raising up a company of sons and daughters in the earth who have taken a radical stand for consecration and holiness. Their secret is not found in legalism or duty, but rather in that they have learned how to live in Christ. Consecrated ones know their identity in God and walk upright before Him. They not only establish a clear standard of righteousness in the land, but they also live it without hypocrisy. Consecrated men and women are often rejected because their desire to live holy challenges other people's desires to live worldly. The call to deeper levels of consecration will always be wrongly labeled as legalism by people who are not in love with Jesus.

In the midst of a tremendous and dark assault upon this generation, God is gathering a consecrated Bride who will be completely devoted to His Son, Jesus. In Hebrew, the word *qadash*, used 172 times in the Old Testament, means "set apart."[1] It is translated into English as "consecration." Paul reminds believers in 2 Corinthians 6:17 of God's call for His people: "Go out from their midst, and be separate from them, says the Lord, and touch no unclean thing; then I will welcome you."

The call to be consecrated, to be set apart, living holy and separated unto the Lord, weaves its way throughout the Old and New Testaments. In Revelation 18:4, immediately before the wedding day of the Lamb and His Bride, John hears a voice from heaven that tells believers, "Come out of her [fallen Babylon], my people, lest you take part in her sins, lest you share in her plagues." Clearly, the invitation to consecration has a solid foundation in the Word of God. In fact, it is a command.

Raising the Standard

Zealous and intense preachers who contend for holiness and revival are initially attractive. Then, those who run with them often become disgruntled at just how hot the fire is, how costly the lifestyle is, and how offensive the message is. Many decide to leave! Over the years, I've witnessed many of them express how much they miss the furnace. They wish they had never pulled back. They wish they could experience the fire again, the way they used to. Sadly, they have fallen back into a typical Christian life.

The bottom line is simple: You can't experience the wonders of the fire without the price of surrender. It's not a seasonal or part-time calling; it's a 24/7 lifestyle of extreme passion and intensity for Jesus. It hurts, yet it's glorious.

One of the most important markers of a genuine revival among the people of God is a deepening conviction of sin and a growing passion for holiness. Revival is a time when people weep over their sin and are consumed with a desire to consecrate their lives to the Lord. With a generation so desperate for revival and awakening, the power of consecration and holiness is absolutely necessary to see heaven come to earth. We must continue to pray for the miraculous and engage in prayer and worship, but the call to holiness and consecration must not and cannot be ignored any longer. Yes, we should engage in miracles, prophecy, prayer, and worship, but we must also embrace the lost art of holiness and consecration in this hour. Jesus Christ is coming back for a pure and spotless Bride, not a harlot called Babylon.

The bottom line is simple: You can't experience the wonders of the fire without the price of surrender.

Repentance Prepares the Way for Revival

It was Frank Bartleman who said, "The depth of any revival will be determined exactly by the spirit of repentance that obtains. In fact this is the key to every revival truly born of God."[2] If we want God to visit America with a Third Great Awakening (or visit wherever you live), then we must prepare the way by preaching repentance to all! How many churches, ministries, and leaders are crying out for revival in America and the nations but are not preaching repentance? We need to get back to reading the Word of God!

John the Baptist had a message that was simple: "Repent, for the kingdom of heaven has come near" (Matthew 3:2 NIV). His baptism was blunt. He said, "I baptize you with water for repentance" (v. 11). His lifestyle was challenging. He said, "Produce fruit in keeping with repentance" (v. 8).

Repentance from sexual immorality is of the utmost importance. Sexual immorality is at the top of almost every list of sins in the New Testament. The book of Revelation emphasizes it as one of Satan's primary weapons against the Church in the end times (see Revelation 2:20; 9:21; 14:8; 17:1–4). If people are continually and habitually engaging in sexual immorality and calling themselves Christians, they are deceived (see Romans 6). Lifting our hands up on Sunday morning and pulling our pants down on Friday night is not okay. Whether you are engaging in heterosexual, homosexual, bisexual, or any other sexual activities, if it's not in covenant, as defined by the Word of God, then God doesn't bless it. He condemns it. It doesn't matter if someone attends a supernatural school of ministry, speaks in tongues and prophesies, has a preacher for a daddy, or is under some false grace teaching—if we are not saving ourselves for marriage between a man and woman, we are selling ourselves to the devil!

Revival is always a revival of holiness. It begins with a terrible conviction of sin. It is often the form that this conviction takes that troubles those who read of revival. Sometimes the experience is crushing. People weep uncontrollably and worse! But there is no such thing as a revival without tears of conviction and sorrow.

Revival and Fruitful Judgment

Acts 5 describes an aspect of revival as God judging the Church for her sin and revival breaking out because of it. Here are four fruits of God's judgment:

1. "And great fear came upon the whole church and upon all who heard of these things" (Acts 5:11).
2. Unusual respect and honor came from outsiders toward believers. The Jews actually regarded them too highly to join them (see v. 13).

3. The fruit of God striking down Ananias and Sapphira as believers was that "more than ever believers were added to the Lord, multitudes of both men and women" (v. 14).
4. Power was released to the Church as people brought the sick into the streets and hoped that Peter's shadow might fall on them (see vv. 15–16).

Revival restores Jesus to first place. In a revived company of believers, Jesus reigns supreme! He is preached about, sung about, worshiped, and praised. The cross and resurrection become central realities in revival. Jesus Christ as the Head of the Church is magnified and honored. Martyn Lloyd-Jones once said, "Revival, above everything else, is a glorification of the Lord Jesus Christ, the Son of God. It is the restoration of Him to the center of the life of the Church."[3]

Jesus never needed to be revived during His earthly life and ministry, because He was walking revival. He was never out of His Father's will. The principle is the same with us. If we continually walked and lived in the presence of God, we would never need revival. Revival comes to bring forth repentance concerning idolatry in our lives. This is God's central purpose. His number one priority is to make sure His Son has supremacy in our lives in all things (see Colossians 1:15–20).

Revival Burnout

Contending for revival and awakening without possessing a personal revelation that God takes delight in you will eventually lead to your burnout, disillusionment, and despair. Too many revivalists and intercessors lose sight of their calling because they lack consistent encounters with the love and affection that

Jesus has for them during their years of waiting for the break-through of revival and awakening.

Yet Song of Solomon 4:9–10 gives us a glimpse into how Christ feels about His Bride:

> You have captivated my heart, my sister, my bride; you have cap-tivated my heart with one glance of your eyes. . . . How beauti-ful is your love, my sister, my bride! How much better is your love than wine, and the fragrance of your oils than any spice!

This is why spending seasons of prayer and fasting is non-negotiable for leaders in the Body of Christ. As we wait and receive from the Father, we recognize that our identity and the love God has for us have absolutely nothing to do with ministry.

I'm convinced that it's in these seasons of no ministry, no travel engagements, no nothing, that God's real work begins in us!

The Bestselling False Gospel of Grace

Do not submit yourself to doctrine and preaching that makes provision for your flesh (see Romans 13:14). In Christ Jesus you are a new creation; the power of the sin nature has been broken off your life, and you have no need for it any longer (see 2 Corin-thians 5:17). You have now been given a divine nature, and the Holy Spirit resides in you to lead you into all truth (see 2 Peter 1:4; John 16:13). The false grace message that has become a bestseller in the Church has taught and persuaded Christians that they should expect to sin daily and even frequently. This carnal thought process and lifestyle is an assault on the shed blood of Jesus Christ and the true power of the resurrection.

In Jesus Christ, it's no longer "we can't," but "we won't." For a born-again believer to claim "I can't break free from this pornography addiction" denies the power of Calvary and the resurrection. It is a lie from the pit of hell. Are Jesus and His sacrifice enough for us to walk in complete freedom, or are they not? Of course they are! He made provision for our righteousness in Him, not our continual and habitual sinfulness (see Romans 6).

Are Jesus and His sacrifice enough for us to walk in complete freedom, or are they not? Of course they are!

I encourage you to connect with saints and Christian leaders who are actually teaching and walking in the freedom that the true gospel of grace provides. These individuals don't expect and plan to sin every day that they wake up. They don't constantly make excuse after excuse as to why their lifestyle looks no different than the world around them. I'm convinced that the Third Great Awakening is going to start with people who sit in church every Sunday actually hearing the real gospel of Jesus Christ and the message of biblical grace for the very first time in their lives. Continual and habitual sin will not be accepted among Christians, and they will be taught that this lifestyle will send them straight to hell. That's what real love would communicate to them.

It's time for a generation of preachers to stop making excuses for their pornography addictions and lethargy toward the holiness of God, and return to their first love. Now is the hour to preach Jesus Christ and Him crucified, and watch the captives be set free. There is power in the name of Jesus to break every chain. I refuse to allow the current trends and practices within the Church and among its leaders concerning sin to discourage me away from what I know Jesus accomplished at Calvary and what happened when He rose from the dead. He is seated at the right hand of the Father right now, far above every principality and power (see Ephesians 1:21). I will not receive any doctrine of demons that is attempting to support and comfort me in my sin. Jesus Christ is the King of kings and Lord of lords, and I choose to bow my life before Him and live in Him. I am the righteousness of Christ Jesus, and I am going to live and act like it all the days of my life (see 2 Corinthians 5:21). Hallelujah!

More on Revival

Revival is not an event; it is a Person revealed. Revival is not just a demonstration of God's power; it is an outbreak of His presence. Revival occurs when we have the same kind of spiritual atmosphere outside the Church as we have within it.

Revival is about releasing God's people into God's presence. Revival is about a preoccupation with the Person and presence of Jesus. It is about the corporate grace of God being on everyone at the same time. It is about a corporate fear of the Lord descending on the Church.

Revival is about stewardship and sacrifice, having all things in common. In revival, there are no personal possessions and no needs across the Church. Revival releases saints to meet from house to house, breaking bread and enjoying the testimony of Jesus as they fellowship with one another.

Revival is healthy marriages and families. It is husbands and wives falling in love again. It is children honoring their parents.

Revival knows no boundaries. In revival, our concept of time simply does not exist!

Taken to Hell and Back

Several years ago, while I was extensively studying Matthew 7:22–24 and asking God for increased revelation, I had one of the most disturbing prophetic dreams of my life. I went to hell and was stunned by what I saw! The verses I was studying say,

> On that day many will say to me, "Lord, Lord, did we not prophesy in your name, and cast out demons in your name, and do many mighty works in your name?" And then will I declare to them, "I never knew you; depart from me, you workers of lawlessness."

In the prophetic dream I was taken to hell, where I saw all these ministers and individuals who had performed miracles, cast out demons, and prophesied. What I was shown next, I will never forget. The Holy Spirit showed me long lines of people behind all of these ministers and individuals. He immediately revealed to me that these were all the people who had received the miracles and prophecies and had at one time been delivered. As I gazed at the people in these lines, He said to me, "Did they not *receive* miracles, prophecy, and deliverance, yet I never knew them?"

I woke up from the dream alarmed and startled. I said to the Holy Spirit, "So, there are not only people who performed signs, wonders, and miracles who will be sent to hell, but also people who received all these things who will also be in hell. Why?"

Immediately, the Holy Spirit spoke again to me and said, "Because those who worked miracles, prophesied, and cast out demons never preached the full gospel of Jesus Christ, which is the message of repentance. They were so in love with the gifts that I had given them that people became trophies and souvenirs to them. When My power would manifest in their ministries, they would tell people that I loved them, but never that they needed to repent for their sins. I tell you that a great deception will sweep over the signs-and-wonders movement in the earth. Beware of the ministries where miracles and prophecies will flow, but the message of repentance is a no-go. You have been warned."

Will you pray with me today that ministers and individuals who move in God's power will not only live a lifestyle of repentance, but also preach it? What if people getting healed, delivered, prophesied to, and told that God loves them isn't the full gospel message? What if repentance and holiness is the full gospel message too?

Consecration and Demonstration

During the darkest and most turbulent days in Israel's history, God raised up consecrated individuals like Samson, Samuel, and John the Baptist to shake His people out of complacency and to confront idolatry in the land. These men were known as Nazarites because of their radical devotion to Yahweh. Their commitment to deny themselves the legitimate pleasures of this life so that they might experience a greater measure of satisfaction in God set them apart from the rest of their generations.

A radical consecration, born out of encountering the jealous love of God in the same spirit as the Nazarites, is our only hope in this current hour. The lack of demonstrations of God's power in the Church today is directly linked to our lack of consecration. God is going to pour out His Spirit without measure to consecrated people who choose to live outside the spiritual mixtures of this world. Are you willing to say yes?

JEREMIAH JOHNSON is the founder of The Altar Global, an apostolic resource center that provides training and equipping, leadership and spiritual development, local church family and fellowship, next generation education and empowerment, and a five-fold global ministry network located in Kannapolis, NC. Over the last fifteen years, Jeremiah has successfully planted churches in Florida (Heart of the Father Ministry) and North Carolina (The Ark Fellowship). Operating in a strong apostolic capacity, Jeremiah builds and disciples elder teams and develops five-fold ministry leaders who are graced to function in the local church and abroad. Jeremiah graduated from Southeastern University with a degree in theology and minor in missions. An author of fifteen books, church planter, and popular conference and television speaker, Jeremiah has ministered in over forty states and twenty-five nations.

2

THE RIPPLE EFFECTS OF REVIVAL

PARKER AND JESSI GREEN

Our family was thrust into leading a revival.

If you want to live a status quo Christianity with a simple ticket to heaven, then don't fast and pray. When we decided to fast, pray, and wait on the Lord, we were catapulted into lives of risk, adventure, supernatural experiences, and revival as a result of our time of consecration. There needs to be a point in our Christianity where we appropriately analyze if things are "working" or not. Working according to the Word of God and the promises laid out to us by the King Himself, Jesus.

Only two years into marriage, with our first baby on the way and a new promotion on staff at an incredible church in New York City, God interrupted us. Why? Because He is allowed to.

Parker, my husband, was fasting for twenty-one days, and I was speaking at a gathering for missionaries. While I was away,

I saw an open vision of thousands being saved and baptized in Huntington Beach, California. The problem was, we lived in Manhattan and had vision and plans to be there forever. As I returned from my trip and haphazardly shared what I had seen with my husband, he quickly ran and grabbed a journal and told me that the Lord had been speaking to him about California as well.

About a month later, we met with our lead pastors, and they confirmed the word. We all cried, knowing that transition was imminent. Then the two-year transition plan we put in place turned into only seven months. Soon enough, we had sold all our belongings, purchased a jeep for ten thousand dollars, and headed west with a one-month-old baby. We decided to start simply and return to the basics of our faith. What did the Gospels say? Who is the Person of Jesus? What is the cost of following Him? How do we make disciples?

"Green Light, the Harvest Begins . . ." (Jessi)

We gathered people in our small apartment near the beach and also began to go to the streets, offering to pray for people. One night, a group of ten of us knocked on every door of our apartment complex (about a hundred in total), offering to pray and share the gospel. No one was saved.

I went to the pier to preach, and no one was saved. We handed out hot chocolate. People thanked us, but still no salvations. If there's a possibility of being anti-anointed, it felt as though we were. The vision seemed like a distant memory as we spiraled into financial and emotional despair, leading a fledgling church and moving in no power.

Yet, we kept praying. We kept asking the Lord, *What are You doing?*

During the summer of 2019, I heard these words: *Green light, the harvest begins summer 2020. Prepare the nets.*

With all excitement and enthusiasm, we began to plan an evangelism conference on the heels of the US Open of Surfing, hoping to preach the gospel to the surf crowd on the beach. (Still not a bad idea!) March 2020 came and destroyed our plans like a clay pot being thrown off Mount Everest. The world essentially shut down because of the pandemic, and so did all hope of this "revival." The venue we planned to use canceled on us, followed by partners canceling, with no hope of us finding a speaker.

In prayer, the Lord told us, *I am not a liar—the harvest is coming.*

As we walked the beach and read John 20 and 21, we felt as if the beach seemed like a good enough place. At this point, even if no one came, at least we knew we were being obedient. Perhaps it would be unto something else in the future.

During that summer of 2020, we had the opportunity to lead a revival on the beaches of Huntington Beach, and the *Los Angeles Times* cried out, "Revival Hits the Beaches of California." The gatherings then became international news as thousands came in from around the nation to hear the Gospel preached for 10 minutes on a $60 megaphone. There on the beaches, they decided to repent from their sins and be baptized and filled with the Holy Spirit.

After three weeks of gathering on Friday nights, dealing with a flood and mold in our house, having a broken car, and living in a hotel room with our newborn baby, Summer, we were exhausted. Things began to culminate when the police were at our door, threatening arrest for illegal assembly. As I held my two-month-old baby in my arms, I had to make a decision: *Would I give up everything for Jesus?*

31

Since then, we have seen revival sustained through the preaching of the gospel, discipleship, baptisms full of the fire of the Holy Spirit, and tent events wherever the Lord highlights to us. I use the word *revival* with care and caution, and have spent the last four years quickly studying revival. I also wrote a book called *Wildfires* to break down what is happening and what we are being invited into.

After the beach revival of 2020, Saturate Global and Salt Church were birthed, and we led our first tent revival in Laguna Beach, where hundreds would decide to be baptized in chilly 32-degree waters. It was here that radical generosity would break open as the needs of single mothers were taken care of.

The following year, as success was rising in California, we decided to move into a 32-foot trailer and organize thousands on a field in Kentucky. In that field, they would then be saved, healed, baptized, and delivered. We continued on to North Carolina and established a place there for a habitation of the Lord's presence.

Jesus is calling you to come, now, on a journey of following Him. A "get your hands dirty and lay down your life" kind of following. I believe that you're going to be healed, baptized, and filled with the Holy Spirit in the days ahead as you read this book. You will begin to feel God move in you during the night as you sleep, or prompt you to share the gospel at the grocery store. Do not resist God. Give Him everything, and receive the life that you say that you want.

Jesus once told the Pharisee Nicodemus, "I assure you and most solemnly say to you, unless a person is born again [reborn from above—spiritually transformed, renewed, sanctified], *he cannot [ever] see and experience the kingdom of God*" (John 3:3 AMP, emphasis added). I believe that we have rarely seen revival historically because we rarely see a group of people who love Jesus more than themselves. We have a nation of Christians who are not reborn from above; they are still living one foot in the world and one foot in the Kingdom, and thus, they are at war within themselves.

I believe the rise of depression, anxiety, and sin inside the Church is because we are living disjointedly. Paul told Timothy,

> But understand this, that in the last days there will come times of difficulty. For people will be lovers of self, lovers of money, proud, arrogant, abusive, disobedient to their parents, ungrateful, unholy, heartless, unappeasable, slanderous, without self-control, brutal, not loving good, treacherous, reckless, swollen with conceit, lovers of pleasure rather than lovers of God, having the appearance of godliness, but denying its power. Avoid such people. For among them are those who creep into households and capture weak women, burdened with sins and led astray by various passions, always learning and never able to arrive at a knowledge of the truth.
>
> 2 Timothy 3:1–7

Is the Jesus you follow the *real* Jesus? Does He confront your sin, heal your pain, and empower you to go and serve others in selfless love? We want revival to come our way, in our city, and to appeal to our comfort zones, but, friend, please hear me: The fire of revival falls on crucified lives. We see in the last days that it looks very much like *these* days. So, what hope do we have?

Paul goes on to say to Timothy,

> You, however, have followed my teaching, my conduct, my aim in life, my faith, my patience, my love, my steadfastness, my persecutions and sufferings that happened to me at Antioch,

at Iconium, and at Lystra—which persecutions I endured; yet from them all the Lord rescued me. Indeed, all who desire to live a godly life in Christ Jesus will be persecuted, while evil people and impostors will go on from bad to worse, deceiving and being deceived. But as for you, continue in what you have learned and have firmly believed, knowing from whom you learned it.

2 Timothy 3:10–14

No matter what the days and years look like, you know and serve God. We get to be part of His mission here on earth. The privilege is overwhelming, when you think about it. It's heartbreaking that even for a moment (or for some of us, years), we have allowed the enemy to rob us of such an incredible opportunity. The power, the miracles, the signs and wonders are on the streets and backing those who will preach the gospel! We are hosting gospel raids on the streets because God is raising up a remnant who can no longer be watchers. They are saying, *Here I am, Lord—send me!* Is that you?

The way that Jesus gathered His very first disciples was through a simple invitation to "come and see." The Greek word for *see* is the word *horaō*, which actually means to behold, perceive, or see, or more properly, "to stare at . . . to discern clearly (physically or mentally); by extension, to attend to; by Hebraism, to experience."[1] Jesus is actually saying to His first followers, "Come and experience everything I am talking about. Come behold, discern, perceive, and attend to the Kingdom life." He's not merely trying to teach them something. He's trying to give them an entirely different experience of living. This is what revival looks, feels, and sounds like—when we begin to experience a new way of life and invite others into that life.

What a Revival Is (Jessi)

Revival is more than a Christian conference. It is the Church, the saints, being awakened, revived, and set ablaze with the Kingdom of God and a return to their love of Jesus. I believe that we are in revival. Charles G. Finney is one of my favorite revivalists. He led the Second Great Awakening, and historians believe that he had one of the greatest spiritual impacts on modern-day Christianity and evangelism. He is known as the "father of modern revivalism." Father Finney tells us what revival is:

1. A revival always includes conviction of sin on the part of the church. . . .

2. Backslidden Christians will be brought to repentance. A revival is nothing else than a new beginning of obedience to God. . . .

3. Christians will have their faith renewed. While they are in their backslidden state they are blind to the state of sinners. Their hearts are as hard as marble. The truths of the Bible only appear like a dream. They admit it to be all true; their conscience and judgment assent to it; but their faith does not see it standing out in bold relief, in all the burning realities of eternity. But when they enter into a revival, they no longer see men as trees walking, but they see things in that strong light which will renew the love of God in their hearts. This will lead them to labor zealously to bring others to him. They will feel grieved that others do not love God, when they love him so much. And they will set themselves feelingly to persuade their neighbors to give him their hearts. So their love to men will be renewed. They will be filled with a tender and burning love for souls. They will have a longing desire for the salvation of the whole world.[2]

35

I notice in our Western churches that we have a slight problem. Finney points out that a fruit of revival is that we desire for our neighbors and the people amongst us to be saved, that it burns within us. Yet in our nation, if you behave that way in church, people will assume that you are an evangelist. This is both harmful and inaccurate. A burden for souls doesn't make you an evangelist; a burden for souls makes you a real Jesus follower!

In Matthew 9:37–38, Jesus said to His disciples, "The harvest is plentiful, but the laborers are few; therefore pray earnestly to the Lord of the harvest to send out laborers into his harvest." Perhaps Jesus is sending us out, you and me, together. God is raising up and anointing workers in the harvest, those who will proclaim "forgiveness of sins through the blood of the lamb." As part of the greater global revival, God is shifting the United States for a massive Kingdom campaign. He is quickly moving around people and ministries for what He is about to do. Do not resist Him.

Here are three priorities God is showing us in this time:

- Raid the cities with the gospel.
- Set aside consecrated spaces for His glory.
- Train and equip the remnant.

We truly are entering into a "no eye has seen, nor ear has heard" *kairos* moment in history. Yet with this outpouring comes more shaking of our religious systems, and more of His glory. People often say to me, "I want the faith that you have." What they don't realize is that it's the millions of decisions we make in our ordinary lives that grow us to be people of extraordinary faith. I don't love and trust Jesus because I followed a 5-step program. I love and trust Him because I've learned to know Him.

The early followers of Jesus were called "followers of the Way." They were marked by living a life in full submission to Christ. It was not their Sunday attendance that made them followers; it was their daily choice to follow, and a life transformed by surrender.

Peter chose to follow Jesus because only Jesus had the word of eternal life:

It's the millions of decisions we make in our ordinary lives that grow us to be people of extraordinary faith.

> So Jesus said to the twelve, "Do you want to go away as well?" Simon Peter answered him, "Lord, to whom shall we go? You have the words of eternal life, and we have believed, and have come to know, that you are the Holy One of God."
>
> John 6:67–69

Are we following Jesus the way Peter did? Or are we following a made-up Jesus? A Jesus who brings us comfort and prosperity as we live out our Christian spin on the American dream? Are we clear that every Christian is called to evangelize, even if you aren't an "evangelist"?

What the Gospel Is (Jessi)

It's hard to share the gospel with others if we don't really know it or believe it ourselves. First Corinthians 15:1–5 is one of the simplest breakdowns of the gospel I can find:

> Now I would remind you, brothers, of the gospel I preached to you, which you received, in which you stand, and by which

you are being saved, if you hold fast to the word I preached to you—unless you believed in vain.

For I delivered to you as of first importance what I also received: that Christ died for our sins in accordance with the Scriptures, that he was buried, that he was raised on the third day in accordance with the Scriptures, and that he appeared to Cephas, then to the twelve.

When we are sharing the gospel with others, it's essential that we remember these foundational truths:

- Because of our sin, we were separated from a perfect God.
- Jesus came in bodily form and lived a perfect, sinless life.
- He chose to die on the cross and take on the punishment of our sins.
- He was buried.
- He raised Himself from the grave three days later.
- He spent time with His disciples and then ascended to heaven.

I already know what you are thinking: *I'm not an evangelist.*

Well, maybe you're not thinking that, but 90 percent of believers are. If you asked most Bible-believing Christians if they're evangelists, they would say no. Then to go further, most of them believe it's the responsibility of someone else to share the gospel.

When I first heard of evangelism, I immediately thought of large crusades, campaigns, big marketing, or screaming on a street corner. I think that for many of us, the mom swinging her daughter on the swing next to us just isn't someone we think of becoming an evangelist to. Yes, she looks a little down, but do we realize in the moment that she needs to hear that God can be real for her as well?

I think we overcomplicate it so that we don't have to do it. Yet if we can truly get a revelation of Jesus' love for us, then we can be the kind of people who refuse to watch others suffer without offering a way for them to find the peace and love that comes only from knowing Christ.

Take a moment and pause to consider: What evangelism opportunities do you have in everyday life?

At work?

At school?

At the grocery store?

Amongst your family?

Think about the people in those contexts. Are they mostly churched? Do they have experiences with other religions? What is their mental state like? What is their home life like? Are you around them regularly, or are you unlikely to see them again? Be aware of and know your audience, and open your eyes to the people around you.

One of my favorite Scripture verses is John 4:35. Jesus is talking to the disciples, who have just returned from buying food, and He points to the fields—likely a reference to the people in the surrounding area who are open to the gospel and ready to believe. He says, "Don't you have a saying, 'It's still four months until harvest?' I tell you, open your eyes and look at the fields! They are ripe for harvest" (NIV). I think we can do the same thing when it comes to revival—always waiting, never obeying.

Take a few minutes and start with prayer. The key to growing in the prophetic and other spiritual gifts is being in God's presence. Ask Him to give you vision for the opportunities you have to expand His Kingdom and reveal His love. What does He have planned for your workplace or school? Is there a restaurant or grocery store that you need to become a regular at? What would your neighborhood look like totally saved? Then ask God how you can be part of what He is doing.

Wired for Story (Parker)

John the Apostle is known in church tradition as "the Evangelist." Throughout the entire Gospel of John, there is one supreme focus. That is the good news that Jesus is, in fact, God.

You might ask, *What does this have to do with evangelism?*

Well, let's start at the beginning. John 1:1 says, "In the beginning was the Word, and the Word was with God, and the Word was God." Pointing directly to Jesus, John is making it clear that the same God who was speaking time, space, and matter into existence was, in fact, Jesus. That the God who formed man out of the dust had, in fact, put on "dust" on our behalf. That the creation, fall, and redemption story that runs through the entire Bible all culminated and was found in the person of Jesus, the God-Man.

So then, how does this bring us to the word *evangelism*? Story, testimony, witness. "What we have seen with our eyes, touched with our hands" (see 1 John 1:1).

You see, every human being is wired for story. My children ask for a story as I put them to bed every night. A good story at a party pulls in everyone's attention. A good preacher, or any presenter for that matter, who can learn to tell a story not only holds the room, but also holds hearts in his or her hands. So what I propose that you do to reach the lost is to keep telling the story. The thread of scarlet that runs through all of history and then weaves you in through the victory of Jesus over death, and to a finer point, over your spiritual and eventual physical death.

Too often, our efforts to reach those far from God are cold, full of nerves, and are conveyed as "salesy." The truth is, you are not the one selling; you're just telling. What does a witness do, after all? This is not a trick question. You tell about what you have seen, heard, and experi-

Too often, our efforts to reach those far from God are cold, full of nerves, and are conveyed as "salesy." The truth is, you are not the one selling; you're just telling.

enced. Think of all that Jesus has done for you. He saved you, healed you, provided for you, came to you when you were a long way off.

I want you to begin to think of reaching the lost, sparking awakening, and shifting culture, wherever and whoever you are, as simply setting the story straight. What does that look like? It looks like an introduction. Go back to John 1:1. What does the first sentence say? In fact, the entire first chapter? Is it an introduction to how incredible the apostle John is? How he "found" Jesus? That his ministry is going well and that the church in Ephesus is really cracking and reaching the next generation? No, of course not. That would work against the intent of the gospel. The entire book of John is an introduction to Jesus. How John was found by Him. How all of humanity was and is rescued by God, by grace and through faith by Jesus.

When it comes to your evangelism, change the frame and move the spotlight. Watch the self-conscious, sweaty-palmed, stuttering evangelism melt away as you introduce people to the Christ who died for them, lives again, and now reigns above it all. Let's do something incredibly simple: Take some time right now and write down the story of how Jesus saved you. If you don't remember it, you should. A marked difference takes place when someone is born again. I hear you—maybe you were raised a Christian and were baptized at five years old. Good! What a story of God's faithfulness! My guess, though, is that there was a point in your life where you surrendered to Jesus and everything changed. Why did you do that? What happened? That's the story you have to tell.

The Person Over the Process (Parker)

Here's my story to help you along the way: I was raised a Christian. At a young age, I was infatuated with the Bible, reading it cover to cover at the age of ten, soaking up all I could. I was obsessed. Then little by little, as it usually happens, I wandered away from God. I was lonely and felt isolated, even many times in church. So the validation of people, especially girls, became my focus.

I was never the type to recklessly engage in relationships. I was always a kind of broken romantic looking for validation from the opposite sex. This, in the end, led to betrayal and being absolutely heartbroken as a seventeen-year-old. Sure, I was young and it was foolish, but it was my whole world. I wept, stayed indoors for days, and was depressed. Finally, a day came when the emotion of it all overwhelmed me like a tidal surge. I wept in the shower, sitting down, and cried out to the God I had read about as a child.

Then, everything went still. Don't misunderstand me—not just quiet, but *still*. I felt the love of Jesus overwhelm me, and I couldn't cry anymore. Peace, joy, love, the Person of Jesus invaded my life and my moment of sinfulness and brokenness.

I like to think that in that shower, Jesus baptized me Himself as I cried out to Him. From that moment, everything changed. I met the Man, Jesus. You can meet Him too.

I spent my whole life before then not being introduced to Jesus in this way, and not really introducing myself to Him either. Do you see? A story moves past the argument. The actual power of a living Jesus is what saves. Apologetics have their place, even a righteous defense of the gospel in culture, but only Jesus saves. The Person over the process.

A Simple Path to Follow (Parker)

My wife, Jessi, and I saw revival on the beaches of California in 2020, and then again in Kentucky in 2021. Then we started a church in North Carolina because we had a burning desire to see revival. As much as another Great Awakening is needed, I believe that on the way, we often miss the point if revival becomes the object of our affection. Revival comes when the Church is infatuated with *Christ* again. It is a returning.

We often introduce people to the letter of the truth, instead of leading people to the Person who is truth. They are all looking for Him, even if they avoid it, look the other way, or think they hate the truth.

If you are struggling now to preach the gospel, tell the Good News, be a light and a witness to others, I have a simple path for you to follow: Fall in love with Jesus again. Remember what it was like to be saved. Go and make the introduction, baptizing those who hear and receive the Good News, in the name of the Father, the Son, and the Holy Spirit.

PARKER AND JESSI GREEN are passionate revivalists and preach the gospel with power, shaking religious systems, casting out demons and equipping the saints to be full of fire and making disciples of Jesus. Together, they lead Saturate Global—a grassroots revival movement baptizing thousands and awakening the nations to the resurrection power in Jesus—and Salt Church in Wilmington, NC. Learn more at SaturateGlobal.com.

3

DELIVERANCE AND COMPASSION: A MINISTRY OF LOVE

JENNY WEAVER

Deliverance ministry is a powerful tool that goes hand in hand with revival and spiritual awakening. As the Holy Spirit moves in our midst, deliverance helps break the chains of oppression that have held individuals and communities captive for generations. When we engage in this ministry with wisdom and compassion, we participate in God's broader work of bringing restoration and setting people free to step into their full calling in Christ. Deliverance is essential for sustaining the fruits of revival and ensuring that spiritual freedom takes deep root in people's lives.

As I reflect on my own journey, a major lesson I have learned about deliverance is that it's not just about casting out demons;

it's about showing love and compassion to those who are broken and oppressed. In this chapter, we'll explore the connection between deliverance and compassion, examining Scriptures that highlight our authority as believers and dispelling misconceptions surrounding deliverance ministry.

Before we dive in, take a moment to reflect on your motivations. Why do you want to engage in deliverance ministry? Is it to prove your strength, or to help others find freedom? Remember, pride comes before the fall. It's essential to understand your "why" and allow God to refine you in the secret place.

As we navigate the world of deliverance ministry, it's crucial to examine the Scriptures that guide us. In Luke 11:20, Jesus addresses the Pharisees who accused Him of casting out demons by demonic power. He clarifies that casting out demons is a manifestation of the Kingdom of God: "If it is by the finger of God that I cast out demons, then the kingdom of God has come upon you." This passage emphasizes the importance of recognizing heaven's authority when engaging in deliverance ministry.

Jesus teaches us that a kingdom divided against itself cannot stand. He refutes the Pharisees' accusation by highlighting the illogical nature of their claim. Demons don't fight against themselves, and they certainly don't promote the gospel of Jesus Christ. This understanding helps us discern the motives behind casting out demons and reinforces the need for a submitted and obedient heart. As we engage in deliverance ministry, it is essential to approach it with love, compassion, and discernment. We should prioritize the privacy and emotional well-being of each individual, respecting his or her requests for confidentiality and providing a safe environment for the person to feel heard.

First Corinthians 13:2 reminds us that "if I have prophetic powers, and understand all mysteries and all knowledge, and if I have all faith, so as to remove mountains, but have not love, I am nothing." Love is the foundation of our ministry, and without it, we are nothing. Jesus' ministry exemplifies love and compassion as He sets captives free. He heals the afflicted and shows genuine compassion toward those who are suffering. Deliverance ministry should mirror this same love and compassion. It's not about showcasing personal strength or

Love is the foundation of our ministry, and without it, we are nothing. Jesus' ministry exemplifies love and compassion as He sets captives free.

using fear tactics; it's about serving and loving God's people, recognizing their brokenness, and desiring their freedom from oppression.

Matthew 9:36 highlights Jesus' heart for people and His desire to care for those in need: "When he saw the crowds, he had compassion for them, because they were harassed and helpless, like sheep without a shepherd." As His followers, we care about people too, as He did, and we have been given authority in Christ to cast out demons and overcome darkness. It's crucial, however, to understand and exercise this authority responsibly. Demons recognize and respect authority, and we should exercise ours in love and wisdom. We must set boundaries and use the authority of Jesus Christ to forbid any harm during a deliverance session.

In Mark 16:17–18, Jesus gives us a clear commission:

And these signs will accompany those who believe: in my name they will cast out demons; they will speak in new tongues; they will pick up serpents with their hands; and if they drink any deadly poison, it will not hurt them; they will lay their hands on the sick, and they will recover.

As believers, we have been given this authority to drive out demons and see people set free by the power of God. In order to engage in deliverance ministry with power and effectiveness, it is vital to cultivate a genuine relationship with God. Knowing Jesus Christ and His power is essential for discerning spirits accurately, operating in wisdom, and ministering with love and compassion.

When conducted with love, compassion, and a genuine desire to see individuals set free, deliverance ministry becomes a powerful tool for expanding the Kingdom of God.

In John 15:5–6, Jesus teaches us that apart from Him we can do nothing. As we remain connected to Him through prayer, fasting, and studying His Word, we will experience His power flowing through us as we minister. When conducted with love, compassion, and a genuine desire to see individuals set free, deliverance ministry becomes a powerful tool for expanding the Kingdom of God. By understanding our authority in Christ, respecting people's privacy and emotional well-being, cultivating a relationship with God, exercising wisdom in discernment, and using the authority of Jesus Christ to forbid harm during deliverance sessions, we can effectively engage in deliverance ministry.

Let's continue to seek God's guidance as we engage in this vital ministry. As we do so, may His compassion flow through us like a river of life-giving water, quenching the thirst of those around us. Again, as Jesus said in Luke 11:20 (AMP),

> If I drive out the demons by the finger of God, then the kingdom of God has already come upon you.

JENNY WEAVER is a wife and homeschool mother. She believes in building families and communities in the Kingdom of God. She is best known for her strong preaching, teaching, prophetic worship, and entrepreneurial efforts. Millions of people have experienced the ministry of Jenny Weaver through television, social media, and in-person events. Her testimony sets her apart!

Once a homeless drug addict and self-cutting Wiccan, Jenny is now a true worshipper and lover of God. Transformed by His renewing power, Jenny's heart is to lead people into an encounter with the Holy Spirit that will also transform them.

Jenny is the founder of the Core Group, an internationally known ministry with over fifteen thousand students meeting weekly for training on the prophetic, deliverance, worship, and other spirit-led teachings. Alongside her husband, Stephen Weaver, they have recently planted The Core Revival Center, right in the heart of Tampa. The focus of the revival center is to train and equip believers to spread the fire of God by activating the gifts of God and releasing believers into their God destiny.

4

THE ZEAL OF THE LORD

ALEXANDER PAGANI

We *ain't never scared! We ain't never scared! We ain't never scared!*" This was the spontaneous battle cry that erupted during my session as thousands gathered on the streets in the heart of New York City's Times Square for the Domino Revival hosted by Mike Signorelli. It was clear, bold, and affirmative that this remnant of Christians would no longer be intimidated, bullied, or silenced by the lukewarm, compromising, seeker-sensitive Church! This battle cry from those in attendance was reminiscent of what the early Church prayed two thousand years ago in Acts 4, when the persecution began. They cried out to God to grant them boldness to continue expanding the Kingdom:

> "And now, Lord, look upon their threats and grant to your servants to continue to speak your word with all boldness, while

you stretch out your hand to heal, and signs and wonders are performed through the name of your holy servant Jesus." And when they had prayed, the place in which they were gathered together was shaken, and they were all filled with the Holy Spirit and continued to speak the word of God with boldness.

Acts 4:29–31

This group of believers in Acts didn't pray for God to stop or lighten the persecution, nor did they pray for the removal of their enemies, haters, or antagonists. Not one breath was misappropriated in requesting protection from God. Instead, a deep conviction hit the early Church as its people counted the cost and cried out to God to put their mission into hyperdrive. Whew! Outside the day of Pentecost in the upper room, in my opinion this second corporate gathering of the early Church is the second most important in the book of Acts. My reason for saying this is because, had God not responded to this prayer in the manner that He did, the trajectory of the early Church in the book of Acts would have been a lot different (I'm assuming). God's immediate response to the believers' prayer in Acts 4 lets us know that these kinds of prayers are approved by heaven, and are available for all believers to pray who will need courage to fulfill God's assignment for their lives.

Zeal Is the Identity Marker

It is my belief that in these end times, the Scriptures from Acts still apply. There is a clarion call to the remnant to come out of the mediocrity of the present-day Church, take up arms (spiritually), and return back to the book of Acts's model of Christianity, evangelism, and expanding the Kingdom. Over the last couple of years, those in the remnant have been finding each other. You may ask, *How?* And the answer is found in one word: *Zeal!* Zeal is gasoline that ignites the combustion within the believer's engine to produce *courage*. Without zeal, the believer/Christian experience is nothing more than having a form of godliness but denying the power. Without zeal, the Christian is reduced to ritualism that is mechanical, dry, and lifeless.

Zeal is the "identity marker" that helps those who are the remnant find each other in this lukewarm and compromised church environment. (Not all churches are lukewarm.) Zeal produces in the remnant an inward battle cry that cannot be contained and that must be expressed outwardly, just as we witnessed at the Domino Revival in NYC's Times Square. Thousands of believers shouting in downtown Manhattan "*We ain't never scared! We ain't never scared!*" (in NYC slang) truly was an inspiring moment to all who were present, as well as to passersby, who were gripped with the fear of the Lord.

I believe God is still pouring out His power upon the Church the way He did in the book of Acts. He is causing the Church's zeal to be ignited by causing an irresistible dissatisfaction within the hearts of the remnant, who want to see the true gospel preached and the authentic power of God manifested to confirm it. The Lord likewise sparked the enthusiasm (zeal) of the exiles during the time of Zerubbabel so that they could continue the work of rebuilding the temple in Jerusalem:

> So the LORD sparked the enthusiasm of Zerubbabel son of Shealtiel, governor of Judah, and the enthusiasm of Jeshua son of Jehozadak, the high priest, and the enthusiasm of the whole remnant of God's people. They began to work on the house of their God, the LORD of Heaven's Armies.
>
> Haggai 1:14 NLT

Now that we see that zeal is an important attribute needed for our Christian journey, let's look closer at the meaning of the word, how it applies in our lives, and its importance during these end times. The Greek meaning for the word *zeal* is "ardent concern, enthusiasm, an attitude or emotion of deep, earnest concern; jealousy, envy, rage . . ."[1] This meaning implies intense devotion or an ardent flame. It is easy to see where the proverbial idiom "he's burning with jealousy" derives from. The apostle Paul encouraged believers in the Christian Church in Rome to become more passionately invested in representing their faith openly by telling them to not become slothful: "Do not be slothful in zeal, be fervent in spirit, serve the Lord" (Romans 12:11).

It's possible that Christians can love Jesus, be dedicated to Him, and even be willing to give their lives to Him, and still lose their first love! Sometimes as time progresses, we notice that some believers are not as emotionally invested as they used to be. Relationships can grow cold, mechanical, and ritualistic if the passion is lost, but remaining passionate keeps the fire burning. Such is the same with our relationship with the Lord. If we don't remain fervent, then a slothful, apathetic, and lethargic version will replace our ardent flame for Christianity, and our stoic expression won't attract new converts; instead, it will cause current followers of Jesus to walk away from the faith. This is why, aside from guarding our relationship with the Lord, we must protect, nurture, and cultivate our passion (zeal) for Him as well. An ardent flame can be easily put out if we fail to fan the flame, or if we quench the flame. The apostle Paul told Timothy to fan the flame that was in him and not to let it go out: "For this reason I remind you to fan into flame the gift of God, which is in you through the laying on of my hands" (2 Timothy 1:6).

You can't fan a gift. This gift was given to Timothy by the Holy Spirit, through the apostle Paul, by the laying on of hands. You can, however, fan your zeal by *using* the gift you've been given. When believers fail to use the Holy Spirit's gifts, their passion for the gifts dwindles.

I remember one time years ago when I became frustrated at the abuses of the deliverance ministry. I decided to take a break from all deliverance. It wasn't long after that when I began to notice that my anointing and passion for deliverance were dwindling. What had started out as a couple of weeks of rest turned into eighteen months as I began declining invitations for deliverance conferences. Families in need and seeking deliverance would travel to our church, and I would pass them off to our leadership. I almost completely lost the desire for ministering deliverance. When I realized that my desire was waning, I immediately began to fan the flame. I threw myself into every deliverance activity, conference, or session that I was asked (or not asked) to do, just to kick-start the engine of deliverance in my life. It wasn't too long before I began to feel the motors of zeal turning and I was back to actively casting out demons.

If you're reading this right now and feel that your zeal is dwindling, the answer is simple: Fan the flame! Follow the instructions Jesus gave to the church that had lost its first love. He told them to repent and do the first works: "Remember therefore from where you have fallen; repent, and do the works you did at first" (Revelation 2:5).

Do again what you used to do to stir up the fire. Stir it up by placing yourself in environments that will ignite your passion and fire for God. Get around people who are on fire, who can be your battery chargers. Stir it up!

Don't Quench the Flame

Once you have fanned the flame and are on fire for God, it's imperative that you guard it from getting quenched. Yes, you can be quenched. "Do not quench the Spirit," Paul urges in 1 Thessalonians 5:19. This verse is encouraging you and me to refrain from putting out the fire of the Holy Spirit. It is saying don't put out the *zeal* of the Holy Spirit, that ardent flame of the Spirit that kindles when we gather or when He wants to do something at any given moment.

I know we like to think that the Holy Spirit is sovereign and that if He desires for the fire to burn, then like Moses' burning bush, nothing and no one can put it out. Yes, in His sovereignty, should He decide to want to keep something aflame, He can. But in reality, our human participation with the Spirit is crucial and key to maintaining the flame. Yes, we can quench our zeal. Yes, we can quench the Spirit. Yes, we can put out the Spirit's fire. Yes, we can quench our zeal and passion to the point that it can be extinguished!

The apostle Paul's warning to the church in Thessalonica was for a reason. It's extremely difficult to get the flame started in the first place, and even harder to remain focused on fanning it in the midst of the world's distractions. Yet when something is actually quenched, it's an even longer process to restart it. The word *quenched* means completely extinguished. Paul is telling us not to extinguish the Spirit's zeal because it will be harder to get back each time. Have you ever seen a fire extinguished or felt your passion extinguished about something? It's extremely hard to turn back on. When my desire for something is extinguished, it's almost impossible for me to get it back unless I make a resolution that I'm willing to go through all the effort I did before in order to get it back.

In its current state, the flame of the Christian Church is almost extinguished. The Church's leaders (not all, but many) have lost their zeal and passion for pursuing the Holy Spirit concerning their congregations. Unless they get it back, the Church will remain at a standstill, and many will turn away from the faith. This is why God is raising up a remnant of intercessors within the Church who are standing in the gap, praying for heaven to keep the Church's fire burning. There's a reason why the priests in the Old Testament were required never to let the lampstands in the tabernacle and temple go out:

> The lampstand will stand in the Tabernacle, in front of the inner curtain that shields the Ark of the Covenant. Aaron and his sons must keep the lamps burning in the LORD's presence all night. This is a permanent law for the people of Israel, and it must be observed from generation to generation.
>
> Exodus 27:21 NLT

On the day of Pentecost, when tongues of fire sat on the early believers' heads, that was the ardent flame of the Spirit (see Acts 2). God was imparting the zeal of the Lord upon the heads of those in the upper room, and it caused them to begin speaking in diverse kinds of tongues as the Spirit gave them utterance. If we keep reading, we see that by the time we get to Acts 4, that fire began to dwindle. The believers knew that if they didn't pray for a fresh impartation of boldness, the zeal would eventually be extinguished. Pray to the Lord right now that if your zeal is dwindling, He would refill you again with the Holy Spirit, as He did with the early Church in Acts 4. God will certainly answer that prayer!

The Source of Zeal

Let's look a little more closely at zeal so we can get a thorough understanding of where it comes from, what it is, what it is not, and how to apply it. Where does zeal come from? It comes from God! He Himself is zealous and is the source of our zeal.

If you look closely at Isaiah 37:32, you will see that God is zealous over Jerusalem and zealous to accomplish His plans:

Where does zeal come from? It comes from God! He Himself is zealous and is the source of our zeal.

"For out of Jerusalem shall go a remnant, and out of Mount Zion a band of survivors. The zeal of the LORD of hosts will do this." For many years, I've read this verse and others just like it, but it wasn't until the Lord highlighted a certain part of the verse that everything changed for me. It was the phrase *the zeal of the Lord.* Not the zeal of mankind, nor of emotionalism, but this verse is saying that the Lord also is zealous. Since we are made in His image and can have (or not have) zeal, it would make sense that the Lord also would have (or not have) zeal to accomplish His purpose! God's desire in this case was for the remnant to escape His judgment toward Jerusalem, so He passionately made it His business to make sure that they would not experience the same judgment as others whom He was sending into exile in Babylon.

In Ezekiel 5:13 (KJV), the Lord's zeal is not categorized, but is more personal: "Thus shall mine anger be accomplished, and I will cause my fury to rest upon them, and I will be comforted: and they shall know that I the LORD have spoken it in my zeal, when I have accomplished my fury in them." Notice that the Lord says *in my zeal*—meaning that this was His personal desire and passion guiding His actions toward Jerusalem.

Unfortunately, in this case it was judgment, but the verse is clear that God also is zealous at times in how He deals with His people. There are numerous biblical references like this to His zeal, but these two we have looked at suffice to show that zeal originates with God.

Put on Zeal Like a Cloak

Once we understand that zeal comes directly from God, then we are to add it to our weaponry in putting on the armor of God. Yes, zeal is also included in the armor that He provided to all believers for spiritual warfare.

Look at Isaiah 59:17: "He put on righteousness as a breastplate, and a helmet of salvation on his head; he put on garments of vengeance for clothing, and wrapped himself in zeal as a cloak." This verse is the Old Testament version of Ephesians 6 in putting on the whole armor of God. The apostle Paul didn't mention the word *zeal* in Ephesians 6, but he did reference it when he referred to "supplication" in the Spirit in some translations of verse 18. This supplication that the Spirit gives is zeal, and it's to be put on like a cloak.

The soldiers of the Old Testament, as well as the Roman soldiers of the New Testament, wore cloaks under their armor. All armor was worn over undergarments and cloaks; no soldier was naked. Without the cloak or garment underneath, the metal would have rubbed against their bodies, causing blisters or discomfort. The cloak provided a barrier of protection. The same with zeal—it protects the spiritual soldier from the burden of warfare.

Putting on zeal like a cloak is like mentally preparing yourself daily to fight the good fight of faith and not give up. Zeal becomes a self-motivator in the face of mediocrity, and it causes you to go the extra mile, as Jesus commanded. A soldier cloaked with zeal can go extra miles. Do you see the parallel? Zeal empowers the life of the believer, but he or she must choose to put it on daily, like a cloak.

Allow Zeal to Consume You

With any good soldiers, the mission their commanding officer gives them becomes their only objective. They become consumed with the mission! I remember when I first began to sense that God was thrusting me into deliverance ministry. I knew that I was headed for a religious fight because during the years of 2010 to 2020 (the latter being when the COVID-19 pandemic began), many in the Church were against the ministry of deliverance, and they weren't going to allow me to bring reform without resistance. So I began to wrap myself (figuratively speaking) with zeal like a cloak, and I began to allow God's mandate for my life to absolutely consume me. I lived, breathed, and ate deliverance until it permeated every part of my life.

This level of zeal was needed to be able to see the Body of Christ reawaken to the ministry of deliverance. Psalm 69:9 says, "For zeal for your house has consumed me, and the reproaches of those who reproach you have fallen on me." In context, this verse is a Messianic prophecy concerning the coming Messiah and His desire to restore God's house to its original purpose.

This prophecy would be fulfilled in John 2:13–22, when Jesus drove the money-changers out of the Temple. I think its fulfillment is a perfect depiction of how zeal should actively play a role in thrusting you forward in fulfilling God's plan for your life. Without allowing zeal to truly consume every part of your being, true reform cannot happen.

What has God called you to do? Are you clear on that calling? Then ask God to spark your zeal to fulfill it and to keep that flame lit.

Unregulated Zeal

In its simplest meaning, being *unregulated* means not being controlled or supervised by regulations and laws. This definition alone reeks of rebellion. Why? Because rebellion is the willful violation and absence of law. In a paradoxical way, unregulated zeal is dishonoring God while trying to honor Him. Nothing does more damage to the expansion of the Kingdom of God than unregulated zeal. It's the virus to the godly zeal that God imparts to His laborers in the vineyard.

I think it's necessary to go over a few of the negative expressions and consequences of the level of behavior caused by unregulated zeal. You might not like what I'm going to say, but I think it's absolutely necessary that I say it: Stay away from being radical!

Yes, I said it! Being *zealous* and being *radical* are not the same thing. One is regulated and self-controlled, while the other is unregulated and fanatical. One time, a gentleman who was a member of my church came to the back during a high point in the Sunday service. I saw him talking with another member and saying, "I'm radical for Christ! I'm radical for Christ!" Then he began jumping around aimlessly. As I glanced over in his direction, I pondered to myself that his radical behavior served no purpose but self-affirmation. It was of no value to the gospel, and honestly, it was out of order since it distracted others from worshiping.

Modern evangelicalism's attempt to break away from dry, stoic worship services has gone to the extreme left of "being radical," and now, years later, people are realizing that such behavior didn't do the Body of Christ any good. On the other hand, being zealous is different. It is self-controlled, even when there are moments where God desires to do something unorthodox! No matter what that might look like, when it's zeal, there will always be a glorification of God and an expansion of His Kingdom.

In Romans 10:1–4 (NLT), Paul is clear in stating that the Jews' zeal had become misguided and that they actually offered God false worship:

> Dear brothers and sisters, the longing of my heart and my prayer to God is for the people of Israel to be saved. I know what enthusiasm they have for God, but it is misdirected zeal. For they don't understand God's way of making people right with himself. Refusing to accept God's way, they cling to their own way of getting right with God by trying to keep the law. For Christ has already accomplished the purpose for which the law was given. As a result, all who believe in him are made right with God.

In the Gospels, you find this kind of unregulated zeal displayed with the Pharisees in their interactions with Jesus. No other group in the Gospels dishonored the Son of God more than the Pharisees, while at the same time claiming to worship God.

Maintaining a Spirit-Led Zeal

To close out our talk about zeal, let's look at three areas that need to be addressed to ensure that your zeal doesn't become unregulated and misdirected. They are *ignorance*, *rejection*, and *stubbornness*. Dealing with these three areas will help you maintain a holy, Spirit-led zeal for the Lord.

Ignorance

I have found that the number one reason for unregulated zeal is ignorance. Church folks don't know what they don't know! Bad theology governs them, or no theology. When a believer isn't grounded on the Scriptures, he or she tends to lean toward being experience-driven rather than being Scripture-led. The apostle Paul states in Romans 10:3 that the Jews lack understanding. A number of Bible versions phrase it as "being ignorant," meaning that they didn't have a thorough understanding of the Scriptures. This led to their bad theology, and bad theology leads to bad behavior.

When a person who is zealous places a high value on Scripture, he or she becomes a weapon in God's hands and can be a blessing to the Kingdom.

Zeal is birthed by a thorough understanding of the Scriptures, whereas radicalness is born by bad theology. If you're going to be used by God in what He has called you to do, then you're going to have to become well-versed in Scripture. It pleases God to use sharp vessels rather than dull ones. When a person who is zealous places a high value on Scripture, he or she becomes a weapon in God's hands and can be a blessing to the Kingdom. Apollos was one such believer:

> Now a Jew named Apollos, a native of Alexandria, came to Ephesus. He was an eloquent man, competent in the Scriptures. He had been instructed in the way of the Lord. And being fervent in spirit, he spoke and taught accurately the things concerning Jesus, though he knew only the baptism of John. He began to speak boldly in the synagogue, but when Priscilla and Aquila heard him, they took him aside and explained to him the

way of God more accurately. And when he wished to cross to Achaia, the brothers encouraged him and wrote to the disciples to welcome him. When he arrived, he greatly helped those who through grace had believed, for he powerfully refuted the Jews in public, showing by the Scriptures that the Christ was Jesus.

Acts 18:24–28

Stay away from ignorance, and allow your zeal to be mature by your immersion in Scripture.

Rejection

Too often, those with misguided zeal are overcome by preconceived or self-imposed rejection, just like the Jews who refused to correct their theology and actions. This group also refuses any type of accountability. They view everything as persecution or rejection because of their hyper-expression of their faith. They are quick to assume that the Church is rejecting them because its members are religious or lukewarm. They also reject being challenged to correct their views to a more accurate version of Scripture. They therefore remain in ignorance, which in turn causes them to express their faith in a version that isn't outlined in Scripture, but is more sensational. The Jews likewise had refused to accept God's way, and as a result, they chose a form of worship that God had not sanctioned.

I recently encountered such a person when I went to minister at an event hosted by one of my churches. This person wasn't part of our church network, but joined us for worship and began walking around the church while waving a flag. We normally have our flag-and-dance ministry waving flags, but this person, in unregulated zeal, felt like joining the worship by flagging individually in a highly distracting manner. Our host pastors didn't know this person, so much of the service was spent trying to stop the display of unregulated zeal. The more we tried to control the person, the more this individual rejected our correction and became even more unregulated. It was very frustrating!

Here's a word of advice: When you're visiting a local church where you're not a member, submit to the rules of the house instead of making up your own rules. Any rejection of the house rules is the kind of zeal without knowledge that Paul frowned upon!

Stubbornness

Stubbornness is refusing to change even when the need to change is obvious. The Jews' misdirected zeal was upheld by their stubbornness in refusing to change. Over the long term, unregulated zeal becomes idolatry. As the prophet Samuel told Saul in 1 Samuel 15:23, "For rebellion is as the sin of divination, and presumption is as iniquity and idolatry. Because you have rejected the word of the LORD, he has also rejected you from being king."

You can idolize your own way of thinking—or even idolize your zeal, passion, and how intensely you serve God—so much that you lose the fruits of the Spirit like peace and self-control. You can become driven instead of being led. When this happens, you become radical for the sake of being radical! You do things on purpose instead of allowing your purpose to define your actions. Ultimately, this will lead to a life of stubbornness that will be hostile to the brethren and churches around you. Stubborn people end up getting kicked out of every church, or they choose to church hop and never join a local fellowship. The Pharisees never submitted to Christ, yet they claimed to be waiting for the coming Christ.

Stay away from stubbornness, and allow the Holy Spirit to anoint your life with Spirit-led zeal that is beautiful both to witness and to partake of. Right now, ask the Holy Spirit to search your heart and set you ablaze with His zeal so that you may be counted worthy to be part of the end-time remnant.

ALEXANDER PAGANI is the founder of Amazing Church in Bronx, New York. He is an apostolic Bible teacher with keen insight into the realm of the demonic, generational curses, and deliverance. An internationally sought-after conference speaker, he takes an uncompromising approach to the Scriptures and has been involved in thousands of deliverance sessions. He has appeared on various television networks, including TBN, The Word Network, and others. An honorary graduate of Central Pentecostal Bible Institute, he carries a spirit of wisdom and discernment to unlock secrets of the kingdom with signs and wonders following his ministry. He currently lives in the Metro-Atlanta area with his wife, Ibelize, and their sons, Apollos and Xavier.

5

REVIVAL AND EVANGELISM: THE DIVINE PARTNERSHIP

ISAIAH SALDIVAR

The Church is sleepwalking in a haze of comfortable Christianity. We warm chairs on Sunday morning, sing our favorite songs, hear a feel-good message, and leave exactly the same as we came. According to polls, 61 percent of Christians haven't shared their faith in the last six months.[1] Most believers have never led another person to Christ. We've replaced the fire of revival with the comfort of religion, and we've traded the Great Commission for great complacency.

Let me be direct: This is not biblical Christianity. This is not the gospel Jesus preached. This is not what the early Church demonstrated in the book of Acts. We live in desperate times but remain silent, more concerned about our comfort than others' eternal destiny.

We carry the cure for eternal death in our pockets, yet we walk through a cancer ward without sharing it. We have the answer to humanity's greatest need, yet we remain silent. Why? Because we're afraid of looking weird. We're so scared of feeling uncomfortable. We're afraid of what people might think.

But God is doing something new in this hour. He is raising up a generation that is running after both the fire of revival and the harvest of evangelism. He is breaking the spirit of fear that has muzzled His Church, and is calling His people back to the raw power of biblical Christianity.

The Divine Disruption

Something powerful happens when revival and evangelism collide. At nineteen years old, I was an atheist. Every other word out of my mouth was profanity. I had my life perfectly planned—I was about to become a police officer, get engaged to my girlfriend of four years, and graduate college early with my degree. I wanted nothing to do with God.

But God had other plans.

My sister kept inviting me to church. For eight months she persisted, until finally I agreed to go, just to shut her up. On January 12, 2011, I walked into that sanctuary, declaring, *God, I don't want anything to do with You. I'm never coming back after today.*

What happened next shattered my atheism and launched me into a dimension I didn't even know existed. During worship, I felt something physically pulling on my shirt. Not emotionally or metaphorically—physically. There I was, sitting in the back of a 3,000-seat sanctuary, and the tangible presence of God was tugging at me like a child trying to get a parent's attention.

70

I ran to that altar and made a deal with God: *If You prove You're real, I'll give You everything. I'll move out of state. I'll travel the world. I'll break up with my girlfriend.*

Then it happened—an audible voice from heaven declared, "Isaiah, I don't want 99.9 percent of you. I want *all* of you. I'm going to use you."

For the next three days, I didn't sleep. For the next two weeks, I didn't eat. I was seeing angels and demons everywhere. Physical dirt came out of my eyes as spiritual scales fell away. My family thought I had lost my mind—and maybe I had. I had lost my natural mind to gain the mind of Christ.

The Pattern of Divine Disruption

This wasn't just my experience; it was a biblical pattern. Look at Saul on the road to Damascus, knocked off his horse by the glory of God. Look at Isaiah in the temple, undone by a vision of God's holiness. Look at John on the island of Patmos, falling as dead before the risen Christ.

When revival truly hits, it disrupts everything. It's not a gentle suggestion to adjust your lifestyle; it's a divine invasion that rearranges your entire existence.

When revival truly hits, it disrupts everything. It's not a gentle suggestion to adjust your lifestyle; it's a divine invasion that rearranges your entire existence.

The problem with much of modern Christianity is that we've tried to tame this disruption. We've attempted to domesticate the divine to fit it neatly into our Sunday schedule.

But genuine revival doesn't ask permission to disrupt your plans. It doesn't negotiate with your comfort zone. It doesn't respect your religious traditions. Revival is God Himself stepping into time and space, revealing His glory so that everything else becomes secondary.

With me, things quickly went from personal revival to a corporate awakening. Within days of my conversion, God gave me a mandate: *If you'll pray and consecrate your life, I'll break out an organic, grassroots revival in your living room like America has never seen.*

I had no theological framework for revival. I hadn't read the Bible yet. I just knew God had spoken. So I invited my party friends over. Instead of drugs and alcohol, they encountered the power of God. People were getting delivered from demons. Bodies were being healed. Lives were being transformed. In the first week, 30 people showed up. The following week, 60. Then 90, then 120. Within three to four months, 400 to 500 people were crammed into my house.

This wasn't about slick marketing. We had no social media, no flyers, no advertising. It wasn't about professional programming. We had no worship band, no fog machines, no light shows. This was purely the presence of God drawing people to Himself.

People would arrive at 8 a.m. for a 7 p.m. service, just to get a spot inside. Others would stand outside, looking in through the windows. I would stand in one spot, unable to move, preaching until I was blue in the face. This wasn't polished preaching; this was a raw encounter with the living God.

The Ripple Effect of Authentic Revival

What started in my living room quickly began to impact entire families and communities. My brother, one of the biggest drug dealers in our area, was about to open a drug house in

San Francisco. Instead, he encountered God and now has three Christian albums and runs a successful business.

My sister became a lawyer.

My parents got saved.

The ripple effect continued to spread.

We find this pattern repeated over and over in Scripture. When the Holy Spirit fell in the upper room, He didn't stay contained there (see Acts 2). Those 120 people burst into the streets, and 3,000 people were saved in one day. True revival cannot be contained; it inherently leads to evangelism.

But let me be clear about something: I'm not talking about cheap evangelism. I'm not talking about getting people to repeat a prayer and then abandoning them to figure out Christianity on their own. This is one of the greatest mistakes in modern evangelism. The problem with modern evangelism is that the sinner's prayer has become one of the greatest deceptions in the Church, particularly in my country of America. Nowhere in Scripture do we see this formula of "repeat after me, and you're saved." In the Bible, we see radical conversions that led to radical discipleship.

When Jesus called people, He said, "If anyone comes to me and does not hate his own father and mother and wife and children and brothers and sisters, yes, and even his own life, he cannot be my disciple" (Luke 14:26). He wasn't suggesting a casual commitment; He was calling for complete surrender.

I've heard too many evangelist friends say, "Oh, I just led my Uber driver to Christ!" Yet all they did was get someone to repeat a prayer. That's not biblical evangelism. That's not what we see in the New Testament. That's not what produces lasting fruit.

The Marriage of Revival and Evangelism

Here's what happens when revival power meets genuine evangelism:

1. *Supernatural conviction*
   When revival meets evangelism, we don't have to convince people that they're sinners. The Holy Spirit does the heavy lifting. I've seen people walk into revival meetings and fall to their knees before anyone says a word. Why? Because the presence of God makes sin uncomfortable. The same presence that draws also exposes.

2. *Demonstrative power*
   In true revival evangelism, we don't just preach the gospel. We demonstrate it. Jesus said in Mark 16:17–18, "And these signs will accompany those who believe: in my name they will cast out demons; they will speak in new tongues; they will pick up serpents with their hands; and if they drink any deadly poison, it will not hurt them; they will lay their hands on the sick, and they will recover."

3. *Immediate activation*
   When people get genuinely saved in revival, they immediately become evangelists themselves. They can't help it! They're so overwhelmed by what God has done that they have to tell others. I've seen new converts leading their entire families to Christ within days of their salvation.

Let me be honest with you—this kind of ministry costs everything. When revival and evangelism merge, it demands your whole life. You can't schedule it. You can't control it. You can't maintain a comfortable American lifestyle and carry this level of power.

In our living room revival, I would preach until 2 a.m., get up at 6 a.m. to pray, go to work, come home to people waiting for prayer, and do it all again. My schedule was hijacked by heaven. My plans were interrupted by divine appointments. My comfort was sacrificed on the altar of obedience.

But here's what I've learned: What God asks you to lay down, He gives back multiplied. Yes, I broke up with my girlfriend over text messaging (not recommended, by the way). Yes, I gave up my law enforcement career. Yes, I looked foolish to my family and friends. But God has given me more than I could have imagined: a ministry that spans the globe, thousands of souls in the Kingdom, and the privilege of being part of a genuine revival.

Practical Keys to Revival Evangelism

Let me give you some practical keys for stepping into this divine partnership of revival and evangelism. But before I do, let me be clear that these aren't formulas. You can't reduce the supernatural to a system. There are biblical principles, however, that position us for divine encounter and effective ministry.

1. *Develop a prayer life that scares religious people.*
   I'm not talking about saying grace over your food or mumbling a quick prayer before bed. I'm talking about the kind of prayer that loses track of time. When I first got saved, I would go into my prayer closet at 9 a.m. thinking I'd pray for fifteen minutes, and I'd come out at 2 p.m. I wasn't sleeping; I was caught up in the presence of God!

   The Bible says in Jeremiah 29:13, "You will seek me and find me, when you seek me with all your heart." Notice it doesn't say "with all your convenience" or "with all your spare time." It says "with all your heart." You might need to delete some apps off your phone, cancel some Netflix subscriptions, and create space for extended prayer.

Listen, if you can binge-watch an entire season of your favorite show but can't pray for an hour, you don't have a time problem; you have a hunger problem.

2. *Master your testimony.*

Your testimony is one of your most powerful evangelistic tools. The man born blind in John 9 didn't know much theology, but he said, "One thing I do know. I was blind but now I see!" (v. 25 NIV). Nobody could argue with his experience.

Here's how to structure your testimony for maximum impact. First, start with the pain point. What was your life like before Christ? Don't glorify sin, but be honest about your struggles. People need to relate to your story. Second, share the divine intersection. What happened when you encountered God? Be specific. Again, don't use religious jargon. Tell it the way you'd tell it to a friend who has never been to church. Finally, as you share your testimony, show the transformation. What's different now? Not just what you stopped doing, but what you started experiencing. Peace, joy, purpose, power—these are things every human heart longs for.

3. *Learn to read the room spiritually.*

Jesus never ministered to two people exactly the same way. Why? Because He could discern what the Father was doing in each situation. John 5:19 (NIV) says, "The Son can do nothing by himself; he can do only what he sees his Father doing."

In our living-room revival, I learned to recognize different types of atmospheres:

- Breaking atmospheres: When there's thick resistance, and you need to press through in worship and warfare
- Healing atmospheres: When faith is high, and miracles flow easily
- Deliverance atmospheres: When demons start manifesting without anyone even laying hands on people
- Glory atmospheres: When God's presence is so thick that you can hardly stand

Each atmosphere requires different responses and different approaches to ministry.

4. *Build a culture of supernatural expectation.*

Here's what kills most revival moves: People get used to God's presence. They start taking the supernatural for granted. What was once extraordinary becomes normal, and not in a good way.

In our meetings, we cultivated constant expectation in a few specific ways. First, we documented every miracle. We kept detailed records of healings, deliverances, and salvations. We also shared fresh testimonies. We didn't just rehash old stories, but shared what God was doing in the moment. In addition to this, we created space for God to move. It's tempting to fill every moment with activity or have a full agenda for our services. But we need to make intentional time and space for God to move. Finally, we trained people to minister. Everyone got to participate in ministry, not just the leaders.

5. *Develop a warfare mindset.*

When you step into revival evangelism, you're declaring war on hell. The enemy doesn't give up territory easily.

You'll often face religious opposition from other Christians uncomfortable with power ministry. You'll also encounter personal attacks on your mind, body, relationships, and finances. In addition, you may experience spiritual warfare, which is direct demonic resistance to what God is doing.

But here's the key—you're not fighting *for* victory; you're fighting *from* victory. Jesus already won. We're just enforcing His triumph.

Sustaining Revival and Evangelism Long-Term

One of the biggest things people need to correct is treating revival like an event rather than a lifestyle. They want the excitement of supernatural encounters but aren't willing to build the foundation for a sustained move of God. Let me show you what it takes to maintain revival fire and evangelistic effectiveness over the long haul. Specifically, let's look more closely at establishing a daily "revival rhythm," building sustainable structures, protecting God's presence, and counting the cost of continuation.

Establishing a Daily "Revival Rhythm"

First, you need to establish a daily "revival rhythm" in your personal life. When our living-room meetings were at their peak, I discovered that maintaining God's presence wasn't about huge emotional experiences, but about daily faithfulness in the secret place.

The foundation of this rhythm begins before sunrise. Start your day in God's presence before you touch your phone. I'm not legalistic about times, but I am passionate about priorities. If you're checking Instagram before checking in with heaven, you're already behind. This morning communion with God sets the tone for everything that follows.

Throughout the day, maintain what Paul called "praying without ceasing" (see 1 Thessalonians 5:17). This isn't about being in a prayer closet 24/7; it's about maintaining an open line of communication with God throughout your day. I'm constantly asking, *Holy Spirit, what are You doing right now? Whom do You want me to talk to? What's my assignment at this moment?* This continuous dialogue keeps you sensitive to divine appointments and supernatural opportunities.

As the day closes, take time for reflection and evaluation. Ask yourself, *What did God do today? Where did I miss Him? What do I need to adjust for tomorrow?* This isn't about condemnation; it's about staying sensitive to His leading and building on each day's experiences.

Building Sustainable Structures

While revival itself can't be programmed, we need structures to steward it. Think about rivers—they need banks to flow effectively. Without structure, even the most powerful move of God can become scattered and ineffective.

In our revival, we learned quickly that new converts needed clear paths for growth. We developed comprehensive discipleship systems that began with identity before rushing people into ministry. New believers were integrated into small group communities where they could find accountability and support. As they grew, we provided ministry training opportunities that allowed them to step into their callings.

Leadership development became crucial as the revival grew. We could only sustain the movement by multiplying workers for the harvest. This meant identifying emerging leaders and giving them real opportunities to minister. We provided honest feedback and correction when needed, and then released them to their assignments when they were ready. This wasn't a formal program; it was spiritual parenting that produced spiritual multiplication.

The administrative side of revival might not be exciting, but it's vital. We developed systems for following up with new converts, documenting testimonies and miracles, maintaining financial accountability, and communicating with our growing community. Many precious souls would have slipped through the cracks without these practical structures.

Protecting God's Presence

One of the most critical aspects of sustaining revival is protecting the presence of God. In the Old Testament, they had to keep the fire burning on the altar continuously (see Leviticus 6:13). Someone had to tend, feed, and watch over it. This principle remains true today.

Sin must be dealt with quickly and thoroughly. When issues arose in our meetings, we addressed them immediately, and publicly if necessary. Acts 5 shows us that God takes holiness seriously in revival contexts. The presence of God is like a precious treasure that must be guarded with vigilance and valor.

Familiarity poses another serious threat to sustained revival. When the supernatural becomes routine, we risk becoming casual with the King of kings. I've watched powerful moves of God dwindle because people lost their reverence while attempting to maintain intimacy. True intimacy with God should increase our awe, not diminish it.

Perhaps the most significant key to protecting the presence is staying hungry. The moment you think you've "arrived" is the moment you begin to decline. I've seen too many people who experienced genuine revival become satisfied with memories instead of pressing in for more. Yesterday's manna won't feed today's hunger. Each day requires fresh bread from heaven.

Counting the Cost of Continuation

Sustaining revival and evangelism is exhausting. It will cost you everything—continuously. When you think you've paid the full price, God will ask for more.

The nights I felt least qualified, least prepared, and least able were often the nights God moved most powerfully. Why? Because when we come to the end of ourselves, we create space for God to show up in His fullness. Our weakness becomes the stage for His strength.

The key to sustainability isn't finding balance in the natural sense—it's finding supernatural rhythm. There will be seasons of intense output, followed by seasons of divine restoration. The mistake many make is trying to moderate the intensity of their response to God to make it more manageable. Instead, we need to learn to ride the waves of God's timing, giving everything in the moments He demands it, and then receive His restoration in the moments He provides it.

When we come to the end of ourselves, we create space for God to show up in His fullness. Our weakness becomes the stage for His strength.

This lifestyle isn't for everyone. Jesus was very clear about counting the cost. But for those willing to pay the price, there's a realm of power and effectiveness that makes every sacrifice worth it. I've watched former drug addicts become mighty ministers of deliverance. I've seen broken teenagers become powerful evangelists. I've witnessed businesspeople leave lucrative careers to pursue revival full-time. The common thread? They all counted the cost and decided Jesus is worth it all.

The Prophetic Urgency of This Hour

We're living in a moment that the prophets of old longed to see. Joel 2:28–29 speaks of a time when God will pour out His Spirit on all flesh—not just on the priests, not just on the prophets, but on everyone willing to receive it. I believe we're stepping into that moment right now.

What we're seeing now isn't just another revival; it's part of God's end-time agenda. Matthew 24:14 declares, "And this gospel of the kingdom will be proclaimed throughout the whole world as a testimony to all nations, and then the end will come." Notice the end-time partnership here: the gospel and power working together as a testimony to all nations.

But here is what's shocking: God has to go outside the Church to find people willing to carry this end-time revival. In Matthew 22, Jesus tells a parable about a wedding feast. Those who were initially invited, representing the religious system, were too busy with their lives—their businesses, their marriages, their daily concerns. So the master sent his servants to the highways and byways to bring in whoever would come.

This is precisely what we're seeing today. God is raising up the most unlikely candidates to carry His revival fire. Former drug addicts are becoming evangelists. Former gang members are leading prayer movements. Recovered alcoholics are seeing miracles flow through their hands. Former atheists like me are preaching the gospel, with signs and wonders following. Why? Because we have nothing to protect, no religious reputation to maintain, and no theological system to defend. We're just grateful that God saved us and desperate enough to do whatever He asks.

The Divine Disruption of Systems

We're witnessing God systematically disrupting every man-made system in the Church. Traditional religious structures are being bypassed as some of the most powerful moves of God happen in living rooms, parking lots, and street corners. While I believe in education, God is raising up people who encounter Him powerfully first and get their education second. He is prioritizing revelation over information.

The social order is being turned upside down as revival breaks out in unexpected places. We're seeing outbreaks of God's power among drug addicts, in prisons, in gangs. God is purposely choosing "what is foolish in the world to shame the wise" (1 Corinthians 1:27).

This isn't just about reaching people; it's about completely dismantling our preconceptions about how God works. We don't have time to play Church anymore. Approximately 150,000 people die every day, most without knowing Jesus.[2] We are one generation away from potential spiritual extinction in many nations. This isn't about building our ministries or platforms. This is about the harvest.

Jesus said in John 4:35, "Do you not say, 'There are yet four months, then comes the harvest'? Look, I tell you, lift up your eyes, and see that the fields are white for harvest." The time for waiting is over. The time for preparation is over. The fields are white right now, but we need workers who carry both the fire of revival and the passion for souls.

As you read this, you may be feeling a stirring in your spirit. You know that God is calling you to more than comfortable

Christianity. You're tired of playing it safe. You're dissatisfied with church as usual.

That stirring is an invitation. You have a role in this hour! God is looking for those who will pay the price for revival, who will step out of comfort into commission, who will leave the shallow waters of religion for the deep waters of power.

The invitation is going out right now, but just like in the parable of the wedding feast, many will be too busy, too comfortable, and too distracted to respond. The choice before you is clear: Will you continue in comfortable Christianity, or will you answer the call to carry both His presence and His message?

A Final Challenge

The marriage of revival and evangelism isn't optional in this hour. It's not for a select few. It's God's standard for normal Christianity. The world doesn't need another dead church service or powerless sermon. People don't need another religious program or man-made revival.

The world needs to encounter the same Jesus who turned water into wine, opened blind eyes, raised the dead, and set captives free. And He's still doing it today. The same revival power that shook my living room is available right now. The same Holy Spirit who fell at Pentecost wants to fall in your life. The same Jesus who sent out disciples with power to heal the sick and cast out demons wants to send you.

The only question is, Will you respond? Will you say yes to the inconvenience of His calling? Will you embrace the cost of carrying His presence? Will you accept the responsibility of reaching the lost? Will you pay the price of sustained revival?

The harvest is waiting. Heaven is watching.

What's your answer?

ISAIAH SALDIVAR saw his life transformed in an instant when he accepted Christ in 2011. He sensed a call to preach the gospel to every nation and today travels and preaches a message of revival and repentance, having spoken in more than five hundred churches, and at conferences and other events. His attention for the last several years has been reaching people through social media, and right now his ministry reaches 6 to 8 million people each week through various platforms. He also hosts a weekly podcast called *Revival Lifestyle* that is currently in the top 1 percent of podcasts in the world. Isaiah also uploads videos every day to his YouTube channel, which currently has over 950,000 subscribers. Isaiah has been married to his wife, Alyssa, for ten years and has four daughters: Justice, Journey, Harvest, and Nova.

6

KIDS IN REVIVAL

MALLORY HAYWARD

As I write this, it is midnight in New York. I am sitting here trying to brainstorm the best way to explain to you what revival looks like in children, but all I can think about is how I'm trying to fit revival into my own home. Some days, it doesn't feel as though there's an active revival in my home. Sometimes, it feels like housework, stress, and overstimulation all crammed into a small apartment with twin boys, both diagnosed with autism, while I try to navigate everything at once.

You see, you are not alone as a parent, and parenting surely didn't come with a manual. But as I was meditating on the word *revival*, I felt the very breath of the Holy Spirit fill my lungs, to be used to breathe life back into you! The Holy Spirit spoke to me and said, *Revival is a movement.*

Revival is failing forward and moving forward. Revival is the catalyst that forces people to make a choice: *Am I going to*

87

go all in for Jesus, or stay on the fence? Revival is a choice we must make every single day. Revival isn't a "three-step method" or a "manual." Revival is continually dying to your flesh and releasing your wants and needs, to ask God for His wants and needs for you and for your family. Revival isn't a jump-and-dance worship session for forty-eight hours, and then it's over. Revival is a daily choice to crucify your flesh and yield to the Holy Spirit, day after day after day after day.

What does that mean for us as parents? The enemy wants to shift your focus and distract you with stress, worry, perfectionism, escapism, mom or dad guilt, doctor diagnoses, or simply defeat. Yeah, me too. There's not a day that goes by when I don't have to take my thoughts captive and tell my mind to align with the Word of God. You are not alone. Revival in your home is constantly saying out loud, *Okay, God, You are welcome here. I need You to show up because I cannot do this in my own strength.*

Revival in your home is modeling humility and teaching your children that you need Jesus every single day. Your children are looking to you to show them the way. It's time to speak the Word of God on your tired days, on your weary days, and on your overstimulated days. Revival starts with *you*!

I decree that a fire will ignite in you right now! God is waiting for you to take the first step and jump into the water. God is waiting for your *yes*. Your time is now!

Get Your Overalls On

Okay, so you are ready for revival. What now? In order for revival to be sustained in you, your home must be like a field of fresh soil, and you must be the farmer. Get your metaphorical overalls on, because it's time to get to work. God is going to give you good seed to plant into your children, and that seed will bloom into a garden!

What does it mean to have fresh soil in your home? When a farmer is getting ready for the harvest season, he must till the ground to break up hard soil and remove any weeds. As parents, we must look into our own hearts and see what needs to be tilled away. What sin in your life is blocking you from a fresh revival in your home? We must deal with the grit that is blocking us from our freedom. We must let God have full control over our lives and homes.

Jeremiah 4:3–4 says, "For thus says the LORD to the men of Judah and Jerusalem: 'Break up your fallow ground, and sow not among thorns. Circumcise yourselves to the LORD; remove the foreskin of your hearts.'" When that Scripture says "sow not among thorns," the Lord is saying that we must be careful where we sow our seed. Are we sowing seeds of fear, unforgiveness, or negativity when we face various trials? Or are we sowing seeds of faith when that doctor's negative report comes in? We must choose to sow the right seeds by creating an atmosphere of worship and praise daily. In verse 4, when it states "Circumcise . . . the foreskin of your hearts," this means that the Lord wants us to really take a look into our hearts. Jeremiah 17:9 says, "The heart is deceitful above all things." This means that it is vital for us to walk in the spirit and truth of the Word, rather than in our flesh. In order to obtain and maintain a circumcised heart, we must ask the Lord to search our heart and reveal any wickedness. Once He reveals anything to us, it is our responsibility to give up everything to choose righteousness through Him.

Blessed is the man who trusts in the LORD, whose trust is the LORD. He is like a tree planted by water, that sends out its roots by the stream, and does not fear when heat comes, for its leaves

remain green, and is not anxious in the year of drought, for it
does not cease to bear fruit.

Jeremiah 17:7–8

Freedom is on the other side of giving up our way and going
God's way. We get to praise our way through the doctor's nega-
tive reports. We get to command all fear to go, in the name of
Jesus! We get to break generational curses over our children's
lives by choosing to stop sinning. It is time to walk into our
God-given freedom!

I believe in you as a parent, and most importantly, God believes in you and is rooting for you. Revival is on the other side
of your *yes*. There's no plan B with revival. Revival means never
quitting when it gets hard. It is having faith that God will use
your children for such a time as this. Revival is for the desperate, the ragamuffins, the parents who say, *I have nothing left
and nowhere else to turn to. I can't go back to my old ways; I
have to push into this next level and birth revival in my home.*

Revival comes to your house when you ask the Lord to bring
heaven down into your home so you can take it everywhere
your feet go. You will become not just hearers of the Word,
but doers also, and plant seeds to the north, east, south, and
west of your life.

I believe God is getting ready to do a mighty work in you
and bring a wave of revival to families this year. God is preparing the way for you to know Him on a level you never thought
you could. God is going to use you and your children for such
a time as this. I declare and decree that revival comes like a fire
into your home, and that this fire never goes out! It is time to
build your altar and plant your seeds the Lord has given you—
seeds of revival, seeds of hope, seeds of prophesying over your
children and yourself.

Revival is here, and revival is now. Paul wrote, "I planted, Apollos watered, but God gave the growth" (1 Corinthians 3:6). When you are faithful to plant seeds in a child's life, God is faithful to help those seeds grow and bloom. When you look at how a seed grows, it's never the seed that's capable of growing; it's the environment that seed is in that makes it happen. If a seed is in the proper environment, taken care of and watered correctly, that seed has no other option except to grow. It's the same as teaching a child the Word of God. The seeds planted in a child have no other option except to grow because the Word of God is living and breathing inside us. The right environment of having revival is teaching children the gospel of Jesus, how He gave His life to cover us from sin and darkness. This is the ancient way, the sacred path to having revival in children— planting good seeds inside them.

Active and Sustained Revival

What would it look like if God called you into active revival, but your four-year-old son was just diagnosed with a brain tumor and needed to go into surgery immediately? Isn't revival all about having faith to demand that all sickness and infirmity leave in the name of Jesus, and then it's gone? Isn't revival full of fun feelings of God's glory falling over you, with tears of relief, belly laughter, loud music, and flags? Surely revival can't be happening while you are walking your child to the operating room in silence.

I faced this very scenario. I remember my hands shaking and my chest tightening as I silently pleaded with God to keep my son safe. I was placing all my faith and trust in the hands of doctors whom I didn't even know personally. Surely that can't be active revival, right? It may not seem like it, but what if I told you that this is the very foundation of revival? What if God wants to draw you closer to Him and silence the voice of the enemy that is robbing you from true freedom and trust in the Lord? Revival isn't a feel-good moment, and it isn't a good cry that you needed to get out. Sustained and active revival is moving that mountain in your child's life with sustained faith and trust in God, despite the circumstance. It's taking a deep breath in and a big breath out and trusting God with your child's life.

> *Sustained and active revival is . . . taking a deep breath in and a big breath out and trusting God with your child's life.*

Your children are watching your every move, and they will imitate what you do. Being a children's director at a church for the last eight years, I've noticed a common theme in children: They don't lack faith when you show them how to have it. They simply just believe in their heart, and when they ask "Why?" . . . the answer is enough. They will learn through your reactions and responses. We can teach children active revival through our active responses and reactions to every curve ball that comes our way, every disappointment, every fear, everything.

If you want active and sustained revival amongst children, you must be childlike. You must have unwavering faith like a child. When children have a parent who can be relied on to pull them out of a hard situation, they grow up learning that they will be taken care of. We, as adults, are the children who must rely on our Father, God, to take care of us and our children. If everything doesn't work out according to plan, we find contentment in our heart that we gave our lives to the Lord and that the Lord's way is better than our way. We keep moving forward, and we understand that pain and suffering are part of the plan.

"In this world you will have trouble. But be encouraged! I have won the battle over the world" (John 16:33 NIRV). That Scripture is what grounds me when I am overcome with anxiety and fear. It should be one of the main Scriptures we teach children in active revival, because the enemy hates revival. The enemy will bring forth evil works while we push revival. Are you ready for the challenge?

With God, We Cannot Lose!

You're probably wondering what happened to my son through the process of his brain surgery. How did I hold active and sustained revival through this process of the unknown? I'll explain the goodness of God through some suffering, and with few concrete answers. Leading up to my son's surgery, he had been experiencing seizures that the neurologists couldn't explain. We took him to have several tests, and the doctors thought he might be having non-epileptic seizures, which are seizures that resemble an epileptic seizure, but without the abnormal electrical activity in the brain that defines epilepsy. We therefore thought we might be in the clear—before we had one last test done that was an MRI of his brain. We woke up early, went through the MRI procedure, and felt relieved that it was all finished and that our son likely could slowly taper off his medicine for seizures.

I was so hopeful that all the symptoms were now explained and that my son was okay. But some things in life don't go as planned. The night of the MRI procedure, around 6 p.m., I received a phone call from the neurologist. She explained that Theodore Noble, my firstborn son, had a tumor in his brain and needed to see a surgeon right away. My husband and I stood there as she explained over the phone that the MRI had not gone as planned. The results were not what they had anticipated. I stood there in shock. I could feel my entire body becoming distressed. It felt as if my entire world were crashing down. The neurologist was still speaking, but I could hear a delay in her voice as I tried to understand what she was telling me.

God, this can't be! I've dedicated my entire life to You. I gave my all to the Church. I wake up and go to sleep giving You glory. How can this be?

After we finished the call with our neurologist, we immediately called our family members to express our shock and disbelief. We all rallied together to pray and decree that God's plans are better than our plans, and we gave our Teddy Noble into the hands of his Father God.

As I was trying to reach the very voice of God and process this terrifying news, all I could think of in my mind was, *The devil will not win this.* I looked at my husband and told him that we were ordering a nice meal and that we would set a table amongst our enemies that night. I declared, "We are holding our son close, and we will not give the enemy a foothold in this. We will not give the enemy a fresh cup of water by having doubt or fear! We refuse to let this news deter us from remembering the God we serve. If Jesus slept through the storm on a boat with His disciples, then we will gather around the dinner table, eat a good meal, and put this in God's hands. Victory is ours, because with God, we cannot lose!"

The next day, we met the surgeon. He explained to us that in his professional opinion, we needed to have the surgery to remove the tumor done immediately. This doctor believed the tumor was, in fact, giving my son seizures. We discussed the logistics, and after we finalized our plan, the surgeon looked at me with sincere attention. He went on to say that he was looking through various MRI scans on his computer to do research and maintain his professional knowledge, and when he saw my son's chart, something moved him to call the neurologist who had been working with my son. He asked her, "Tell me about Theodore."

As the neurologist explained what was going on, the surgeon told the neurologist to set up an appointment because he wanted to get Theodore in his room. This surgeon felt driven to meet us and get Theodore into surgery to remove the tumor as soon as possible. There was an unexplainable favor and peace that went before us into that surgeon's room. If you live in New York and have children, you'd know how highly unlikely it is to be seen so quickly. Appointments take weeks upon weeks, with so many moving parts. But when you are serving the Lord, favor just isn't fair and God will find you!

Learning from Abraham's Choice

During the week prior to surgery, there was a stillness and peace on me. There wasn't a voice in hell that could pierce my mind that week. I asked God to have His way, and I smiled through the heavy weight laid upon me. Days passed by, and one day as I was taking a walk and reflecting on the Word of God, I felt the Holy Spirit speak to me and ask, *What happened after Abraham took his son up to the mountain?*

If you don't know the story, let me explain it. The first book of the Bible, Genesis, talks about Sarah and Abraham desiring to conceive a child. They waited a very long time, even after God had promised them a son. When Abraham was ninety-nine years old, he and Sarah conceived a child. God did not forget about His promise to Abraham. As the promised child, Isaac, grew older, God called Abraham to sacrifice this child, to test him. Abraham loved Isaac, but he chose to obey God. So he took his child up to Mount Moriah and began making preparations for the sacrifice.

As a parent, I am imagining every single emotion Abraham may have had leading up to this moment. Every question, every fear, every thought of *Why me? Why my son?* Yeah, I get it. I felt the exact same emotions. What's most riveting about the circumstances leading up to this story with my own son is that the very same week I found out about my son's brain tumor, I also chose to sign the contract—just before that medical diagnosis came in—to contribute a chapter to this book so I could teach about active revival in children. As I reflect on Abraham's situation, I am led to understand that God was testing me too. Was I to take the bait of Satan and believe the lie that God doesn't care about my family, or was I to press in and ask God to have His way in my family's life?

Abraham had to *choose* to have confidence in God and to believe that whatever the outcome was, God's plan was sovereign! The word *sovereign* describes someone who has supreme power or authority. Simply put, God's plans and ways are bigger than ours.

Here's how the story unfolded as Abraham obeyed God and began to set up the offering:

> Isaac said to his father Abraham, "My father! . . . where is the lamb for a burnt offering?" Abraham said, "God will provide for himself the lamb for a burnt offering, my son." So they went both of them together.
>
> When they came to the place of which God had told him, Abraham built the altar there and laid the wood in order and

bound Isaac his son and laid him on the altar, on top of the wood. Then Abraham reached out his hand and took the knife to slaughter his son. But the angel of the LORD called to him from heaven and said, "Abraham, Abraham! . . . Do not lay your hand on the boy or do anything to him . . ."

Genesis 22:7–12

Finally, Abraham lifted up his eyes, and guess what he saw in front of him? "Behold, behind him was a ram, caught in a thicket by his horns" (verse 13). Abraham took the ram and offered it up to the Lord as an offering instead of his son. This parent chose to have confidence in the Lord to provide *before* he saw the ram, *before* he knew the ending to his story, *before* he received a word from an angel's voice from heaven, and *before* he knew God's perfect plan. We had to learn a lesson from him and do the same with our son—having confidence in the Lord to take care of him *before* we knew how the surgery would turn out, *before* a prophetic voice in the church gave us a word, *before* we knew God's perfect plan.

Abraham was a man after God's own heart and trusted in the Lord. He was certain that God would provide deliverance through this situation. Before he took his son up to the mountain, he told his servants to wait and that he and Isaac would be back soon. Abraham knew that God had promised a great nation through Isaac (see Genesis 12:1–2). Abraham stood on the promises of the Lord, no matter what the trial was, because he chose to. As I held my son and walked him down the hall to go under anesthesia and endure a very lengthy surgery, I looked at my family and told them, "Wait here—*we* will be back."

When Abraham took his son up to the mountain, he told his servants that they were going up to worship the Lord there. When I took my son to be put under anesthesia on the operating

97

table, I was taking him to worship the Lord with me. Our worship was trusting in the Lord and in His ways because He has the plans for our lives. I refused to curse God or allow the enemy to violate my mind with worry and doubt. How many of us want active revival but choose to believe in God's plan only when everything is working out? God is asking for our full surrender and our full yes, so that the generation that grows up after us, watching us, will have a radical faith that will not be moved!

I will not be moved by a diagnosis, nor by fear, nor by the unknown, because Abraham refused to be moved. Abraham could have been moved, and then generations after generations would not have been able to lean on this story about him trusting God's plan with Isaac. What stories will ten generations from now say about you choosing to trust God and start revival in your home?

As my son went through surgery, I walked back to my seat in the waiting room, got on my knees, and began to thank the Lord for His plans for my son's life. After that, I waited and waited for what felt like a lifetime, until the surgeon came in and said that everything had worked out fine and he would escort me to see my son. The very breath of relief came to me, similar, I believe, to when the angel appeared to Abraham right before he was going to sacrifice his son. As days passed, my son grew stronger and was soon ready to walk again.

What stories will ten generations from now say about you choosing to trust God and start revival in your home?

As you read earlier, my son had previously been diagnosed with autism, so he has sensory issues and cannot be in crowded rooms. What happened next was something I know was entirely orchestrated by our Father. God gave us a ram in the thicket. The year prior, a very wealthy man had decided to pay for an entire sensory room to be set up in the pediatric unit of the hospital, designed especially for children with special needs. It had been built just a few rooms down from where my son was staying post-operation. The nurses walked in during his recovery and said, "Theodore, are you ready?" They then escorted us to the sensory room, and as we walked into this special place, it felt as though there were sparkles of joy all around us. There was every type of puzzle and sensory toy you can imagine throughout the entire room. Theodore was able to play with all his favorite toys!

The Secret Place

If you are a mom reading this, you know how it feels when you see your child smile and be blessed. It blesses you to see your child blessed. The generosity of this man who donated the special playroom made me reflect on the generosity of God. In His generosity, He gave us His Son, Jesus, who was made a man to understand our pain and temptation. Because of this, we are able to come into a room where God takes off our bandages and we experience His very goodness. After we had gone through the hardest part of our test, we received our ram in the thicket through a wealthy man who was so generous that he created a brand-new sensory space, with every sensory toy my son could dream of! In the same way, God sent Jesus so He could ransom your family. With His life, He purchased the ability for you to step out of the room of accusation, disease, and sickness, and into a play place—"the secret place."

You were born for such a time as this. God is calling you into the secret place. The secret place where you can be a child again and dream again! A place where your faith is no longer moved. As children, we would wake up and look at our parents and say, "What's next, Mom and Dad?" As God's child, it's time to look up at your Father God and ask, "What's next, Dad? What do You have for me, and for my family?"

God loves you so much. God is in this with you, so you cannot be moved. Open up the curtains and let the light in! Give God your shame and past mistakes in exchange for His goodness, which overflows with His grace and mercy. God wants to pull the bandage of shame off you and walk you into your freedom in Him. He is the redeemer of all things. Revival is here for you, and revival is *now*. Your children are about to see a new you! You are the descendants of Abraham and Isaac, and generations to come will speak about your unwavering faith, your worship in every circumstance, and how you chose revival every single day. "Your kingdom come, your will be done, on earth as it is in heaven" (Matthew 6:10).

As I close this chapter, I want to encourage you, just as I encourage the children in church during our circle time: All you need is a small mustard seed of faith. You can come to God like a little child, and the Holy Spirit will come running to you. The Holy Spirit is ready to be invited into your home, your life, your destiny, and your decisions.

If you are a special needs parent, this includes you. God has a plan for your child with special needs as well! I believe that as you open your home to the Holy Spirit, the very presence of God is going to rain down, and your child with special needs is going to feel the power of the Holy Spirit! I believe that revival is going to begin in your home today, and that a fire is going to be ignited. You and your family will become burning ones for the Lord!

I will leave you with a Scripture, because while I could try to write the most inspiring last words ever, it wouldn't come close to how powerful the very Word of God is. Let this be your Scripture that you will stand on to ignite revival back into your home and neighborhood:

> But, as it is written, "What no eye has seen, nor ear heard, nor the heart of man imagined, what God has prepared for those who love him."
>
> 1 Corinthians 2:9

MALLORY HAYWARD is a kids ministry director for V1 Church based out of New York. She is a mother to two twin boys and married her ministry man as they work for V1 Church together. She is dedicated to the local church, her lead pastors Mike and Julie Signorelli, and to teaching mothers how to start revival in their home on all social media platforms.

7

SURRENDER

VLAD SAVCHUK

I once heard evangelist Reinhard Bonnke mention the following story, and it left a profound impact on me:

Once upon a time in a quaint village, there was a little boy who owned a magnificent mansion. This house had two stories, filled with rooms that were adorned with the finest furnishings. One time as the boy was going about his day, he heard a gentle knock on the door. When he opened it, he was surprised to see Jesus standing there. Overjoyed, the boy invited Jesus in and gave Him the best room in the house—the master suite.

The next morning, as the boy was enjoying the new day, there was a loud, menacing knock on the door. It was the devil, who roughly forced his way inside. Determined to protect his home, the boy fought valiantly to get the devil out. After a long and exhausting struggle, he managed to shove the devil out of the house. Tired and worn out, the boy looked up and saw Jesus coming down from the master suite.

"Why didn't You help me?" the boy asked, frustration evident in his voice. "I was struggling with the devil, and You stayed upstairs!"

Jesus looked at him kindly and said, "I am just a guest here in your house. You are the owner."

Pondering Jesus' words, the boy had a brilliant idea. He decided to give Jesus half of the house—the entire upstairs. Jesus thanked the boy for his generosity.

The following day, there was another knock on the door. Remembering the previous day's ordeal, the boy cautiously opened the door just a crack to see who was there. To his dismay, it was the devil again. The devil forced his way inside again, and the boy once again engaged in a fierce struggle to kick him out. After a prolonged battle, he finally succeeded. Exhausted and frustrated, he ran to Jesus.

"I gave You the whole upstairs, half of the house!" he exclaimed. "Why didn't You help me this time?"

Jesus responded with the same gentle words: "I am a guest here in your house. You are the owner."

Realization dawned on the boy. He needed to surrender the *entire* house to Jesus, not just part of it. With a humble heart, the boy handed over the keys to Jesus and asked, "Lord, please take full ownership of this house. Where would You like me to stay?"

Jesus smiled and placed the boy in the best room in the house—the master suite.

The next morning, there was a knock on the door again. The boy started to get up to answer it, but Jesus stopped him. "You're not the owner," Jesus said gently. "Guests don't open doors."

With that, Jesus walked to the door and swung it wide open. Standing there was the devil, who took one look at Jesus and said, "Sir, I must have the wrong door," before fleeing.[1]

This parable illustrates some profound truths about the power of surrender in our walk with God. We cannot experience revival without surrendering our lives to Jesus. We cannot find true freedom without yielding to Him. We cannot fulfill God's call without fully surrendering our will and our lives to His care.

Keeping "Lord" with God

Many of us are like the boy in the story that Reinhard Bonnke shared. We love to give Jesus a little bit more of our life, but Jesus wants all of it. Jesus is our Savior, but He is also our Lord. When you acknowledge Jesus as Lord, you acknowledge His ownership. This means absolute surrender and a willingness to serve His cause.

Satan doesn't mind you being religious, as long as you're not surrendered. He knows that a part-time Christian can't defeat a full-time devil. Think of the first temptation in the garden of Eden. Satan asked Eve, "Has God indeed said . . . ?" (Genesis 3:1 NKJV). Throughout Genesis 2, God is mentioned as "the LORD God" (see verses 4, 5, 7, 8, 9, 15, 16, 18, 19, 21, 22; and also 3:1). When Satan came on the scene, he referred to the Lord as *God*—just God. Rightly so, since God is God, but He is not Satan's *Lord*.

> *Satan doesn't mind you being religious, as long as you're not surrendered. He knows that a part-time Christian can't defeat a full-time devil.*

Before Eve disobeyed God, she first removed herself from under the authority of His Lordship. She took Satan's bait, because in Genesis 3:3, she agreed with the devil's assessment by saying simply, "God said . . ." There was no more mention of the *Lord*. She drifted from under God's Lordship, and it was only a matter of time before she slipped into sin.

We must keep "Lord" with God. Our Savior is our *Lord*, and we must surrender to Him. Again, the devil doesn't mind you being religious as long as you don't relate to God as your Lord!

"Jesus is Lord" was the Church's first theological confession of the Christian faith (see Romans 10:8–13; 1 Corinthians 12:3). In fact, Jesus is called "Lord" much more than "Savior" in the New Testament. He is called "Lord" 747 times and "Savior" 25 times. This doesn't mean that He is not our Savior, nor does it belittle His sacrifice on the cross. Yet this truth destroys the Western idea that salvation is like an insurance card or an escape from hell. Salvation is being rescued from the wrath of God, where we have the penalty of sin removed by Jesus' blood and the power of sin broken by His death. In the future, the presence of sin will be removed as well. Yes, Jesus died for our sins as our Savior. But He lives in our hearts as our *Lord*. Many come to Him for salvation, but don't live in submission to His Lordship. The evidence is clear—while we profess salvation, we also live in sin. The devil, whom we are supposed to trample, seems to be trampling on us. We are called to change the world, but we are busy imitating it. Satan gains hold of people who don't submit to the Lordship of Jesus Christ.

During the Last Supper, when Jesus said that one of His disciples would betray Him, the disciples asked one after the other, "Is it I, Lord?" (Matthew 26:22). Interestingly, Judas said, "Is it I, Rabbi?" (verse 25). Jesus was a teacher to Judas, but to the disciples, He was their Lord. The disciples weren't perfect; they stumbled a lot and even forsook the Lord during His arrest. Judas was different—he didn't have a bad day; he had a bad heart. He betrayed his Rabbi for money. In fact, in the garden of Gethsemane, when he kissed Jesus, Jesus called him friend. Judas treated Jesus as a friend, but not as Lord. He was so familiar with Jesus that he didn't have any respect for or submission to His authority as Lord. Yes, Judas was an apostle who healed the sick, cast out demons, and even had a position in Jesus' ministry—but he wasn't submitted to the Lordship of Jesus. Time exposed that in him. His spirituality was shallow. His commitment wasn't consistent. He was full of compromise.

Jesus isn't looking for more fans; He is looking for followers who will deny themselves, pick up the cross, and follow Him. Fans are fickle; they leave when times get hard. They love the benefits of coming to Jesus but wouldn't pay the price of actually staying with Jesus. Some love to come to the cross, but Jesus invites us to pick up the cross and die. We love to retreat to safety, but we are invited to embrace suffering. Many love to cheer from the sidelines, but we are invited to be in the game. Some love to download the Bible App on their phone, but real followers live out that Word every day.

When Jesus is your Lord, He will use you. But if you are the lord of your life, you will seek to use Him. God will become a means to an end, with that end being some ambitious goal. God must be our goal, not a means to a goal. Jesus is Lord of all our life, or He is not Lord at all.

"That They May Serve Me . . ."

When God delivered Israel out of Egypt, it wasn't just because He had made a promise to Abraham or because the Egyptians were treating them unjustly. While it's true that God had promised Abraham that He would deliver his descendants from Egypt, the primary reason for their deliverance was so they could serve the Lord. When Moses came to Pharaoh, the Lord repeatedly told Pharaoh through him, "Let my people go, that they may serve me" (Exodus 7:16). This phrase is mentioned seventeen times in nine chapters. Moses wasn't lying to Pharaoh to make it easier for the Egyptians to let Israel go. While the promised land was the goal, serving God was the reason for deliverance.

In fact, the Israelites couldn't fully serve God unless they were delivered from Pharaoh's grip. As long as we are slaves to sin, we can't fully serve God in the way He wants us to. As long as we are on sin's payroll, we cannot be fully available to Jesus. Sadly, like Israel, we often don't see freedom that way. We want to be free so that we don't have to live in shame, guilt, poverty, and hurting others, and perhaps so that we don't have to go to hell. Israel probably thought that freedom was about being relieved from the hardships of injustice. God wasn't interested in only removing the enemy, however; He was interested in replacing the enemy with Himself. He wanted to be their Master instead of the monster Pharaoh. He wanted them to serve Him as sons, for they had served the evil Pharaoh as slaves.

The Israelites were better slaves to Pharaoh than they were servants to God. Many people are better servants to their addiction and past lives of sin than they are to God and His purpose for them as His children. The exodus was not primarily to give the Israelites a better life, but to provide them with a better Master. God was to replace Pharaoh. They liked the idea of God being their deliverer, but submitting to Him as their Lord did not come easy for many of the freed slaves. Are you as good (if not better) a servant to God than you were a slave to the devil?

When we think of freedom, it's often about removing something bad. Paul tells us, "And where the Spirit of the Lord is, there is freedom" (2 Corinthians 3:17). There is freedom where the Spirit is present. Freedom is not only when the chains are gone, curses are broken, and demons are cast out. When someone no longer has an addiction, is that when the person is truly free? When a demon is expelled, is that when real freedom comes? If the Spirit of God has not taken the place that sin and addiction used to occupy, then a person is not yet free. People might be delivered from an addiction and a demon, but are they free? If they are not filled with the Holy Spirit, they are not truly free.

Freedom is not about doing what we want; it's about doing what we ought. When you are freed from Satan only to be filled with your own desires, it is bondage, not freedom. Many people get free only so they can live their lives to the fullest. That is dangerous and wrong. Jesus didn't set you free so that you can now erect yourself as the god of your life. Your sins were removed by the mighty blood of Jesus so that you can serve God, at least to the capacity that you used to serve the devil. If you make your life about yourself after freedom, or if you look forward to freedom so that you can do what you want, that's not full freedom. If you switch rooms or pods in a jail building, you are still in jail, even if you are on a different floor. Going into selfishness after being set free from Satan is still bondage.

Most people don't realize that Satanism is based on one big idea: "Do what thou wilt." Meaning, do what you want. Satanism is not just about worshiping Satan; it is about worshiping yourself. When you are the center of your universe, you are more like Satan than you realize. That's where pride and sin come in. In fact, the middle letter of the words *sin, pride,* and *Lucifer* is *i.* When "I" is the center of your life, you are living in pride and sin, and following the devil. That's why Paul said, "I have been crucified with Christ. It is no longer I who live, but Christ who lives in me" (Galatians 2:20). Christ Himself said to His Father, "Not my will, but yours, be done" (Luke 22:42). We must imitate Him.

Develop Your Prayer Life

Prayerlessness is a form of pride. Life without prayer is like boasting against God that you are independent and don't need Him. I would say that the real reason people don't pray is not because they are too busy, but because they are proud and dependent only upon themselves. If you say you don't have time for prayer, stop blaming your busy schedule. Instead, repent of your pride. You will always find time to do what you really want to do!

Pride is the idolatrous worship of self. It's the national religion of hell. That's what made a certain angel of God become the devil. The prophet Jeremiah recorded God's curse on those who placed their trust in themselves instead of in the Lord: "Cursed is the man who trusts in man and makes flesh his strength, whose heart turns away from the LORD. He is like a shrub in the desert" (Jeremiah 17:5–6). Such people will become like a dry bush in the desert, a tumbleweed. No root, no greenery, and no fruit. Busy, but not fruitful. A lot of activity, but no productivity. Life that is not birthed out of prayer is like running on a treadmill, sweating but going nowhere. Prayer is firewood that we must bring to the altar to keep our fire burning. It's impossible to burn for God without putting in this prayer log.

The enemy attacks prayer because prayer attacks the enemy. He knows that he can't stop God from answering our prayers, so he fights hard to keep us from praying to God. When the king made a decree in Daniel's day to stop Daniel's daily prayer life, this servant of God did not budge. He continued to pray three times a day, as had been his determined custom (see Daniel 6:10). Daniel would rather spend a night with lions than spend a day without prayer. Think about that! Sin leads to prayerlessness, and prayerlessness leads to more sin. Being prayerless is a sin. Samuel said it best: "Moreover, as for me, far be it from me that I should sin against the LORD by ceasing to pray for you, and I will instruct you in the good and the right way" (1 Samuel 12:23).

Someone once said, "A praying man will stop sinning, and a sinning man will stop praying." How true is that? What did Adam do when he sinned? He hid from God. He ran from the Lord. Sin causes us to hide from God; prayer helps us to hide in God. One day, God called to Adam and asked, "Where are you?" (Genesis 3:9). God is still asking that question of all of us: *Where are you? Why are you not in prayer?* If you have sinned, run to God for cleansing; don't wallow in sin and guilt.

The flesh attacks prayer, and prayer attacks the flesh. The flesh doesn't want us to pray. Like the disciples in the garden of Gethsemane, many of us yield to the demands of the flesh and sleep instead of praying. We lose the battle with a pillow and blankets. Sooner or later, sleeping saints become slipping saints. These words of Jesus challenge me every time: "So, could you not watch with me one hour? Watch and pray that you may not enter into temptation. The spirit indeed is willing, but the flesh is weak" (Matthew 26:40–41). Do you love Jesus enough to join Him in prayer?

Victory in prayer brings victory in life. Lack of prayer brings defeat in many other areas. Prayer builds up the spirit of a person; prayerlessness only strengthens the flesh. Pray when you do feel like praying, and pray even when you don't feel like praying!

It's a sin to neglect opportunities to pray together with Jesus. Not praying is spiritual negligence, and it's dangerous to remain in that condition.

I find it interesting that Peter slept instead of praying with Jesus. As a result, he received a warning: "Simon, Simon, behold, Satan demanded to have you, that he might sift you like wheat, but I have prayed for you that your faith may not fail. And when you have turned again, strengthen your brothers" (Luke 22:31–32). Previously, Jesus had changed Simon's name to Peter, which means "a solid rock." From then on, Jesus called Peter by his new name, but this time in the garden of Gethsemane, when Peter was caught sleeping instead of praying, Jesus called him by his old name twice. Could it be that when our prayer life goes to sleep, our past life wakes up? If we don't pray, we stray. If we don't watch and pray, we end up with temptations that so often overcome us. Our old life is dead, but the lack of prayer can resurrect it. That's how much detrimental power there is in a prayerless life.

When Satan asked for Peter, Jesus prayed for him, but Peter himself didn't bother to pray. It makes sense why he ended up denying his best friend; his overconfidence led him to prayerlessness, which resulted in him denying Christ three times. Jesus wrestled in prayer, which gave Him the power to resist temptation, but Peter slept in prayer, which resulted in no power to resist temptation.

Not only does the flesh get the upper hand when we don't pray, but spiritual battles in the unseen realm will turn in the enemy's favor. When Jesus prayed in the garden, God sent an angel to support Him. When Paul prayed in the storm, God sent an angel to assist those on the ship. When the Church prayed for Peter, God sent an angel to deliver him. Jentezen Franklin once said, "One of the greatest tragedies of prayerlessness is the unemployment of angels."[2] When you don't pray, God doesn't answer! When you don't pray, God's angels are unemployed. You will fight a spiritual battle alone, and you will most likely lose.

Cultivate a Habit of Fasting

God designed our human body to be able to fast. Did you know that when you sleep, you are fasting? That's why the first meal of the day is called breakfast—it's when you break your fast. So, good news—you've already been sort of secretly fasting all your life! Scientific research tells us that a lot of repairing takes place in our bodies when we fast. The same can be true spiritually. Biblical fasting is not starvation or an involuntary absence of food; it is abstaining from food for spiritual reasons. Fasting is not a hunger strike, and it is not a diet; a diet focuses on helping you lose weight. Fasting restores our hunger for God. Fasting renews our connection to God. Fasting brings a fresh fire of zeal and passion for Him.

Fasting is choosing to be physically hungry for the purpose of getting spiritually hungry for Jesus. It's interesting how that works: Physical hunger done with the goal of seeking Jesus makes our spiritual hunger for Him even stronger. Jesus said that His disciples will fast when He is gone (see Mark 2:20). Fasting is that longing of the Bride (the Church) for the Bridegroom. It's physical pain that stirs spiritual craving for the Lord.

> *Physical hunger done with the goal of seeking Jesus makes our spiritual hunger for Him even stronger.*

Fasting is a powerful way to subdue the flesh. It's not the only method, but it's highly effective. When fasting, you train your body that it doesn't always get what it wants. Your body stops being the master, and the Lord takes control. If you don't defeat the flesh, it will defeat you. Adam and Eve ate themselves out of the garden (see Genesis 3:6). Esau sold his birthright for a bowl of soup (see Genesis 25:29–34). God judged Sodom for pride, gluttony, and idleness (see Ezekiel 16:49). Israel craved meat and faced a plague as a result (see Numbers 11:4, 31–34). Jesus' first temptation was with food (see Luke 4:1–3). Food itself isn't sinful, but gluttony—making a god out of your belly—is idolatry. Jesus taught, "Man shall not live by bread alone" (Matthew 4:4). Paul warned of making the stomach a god (see Philippians 3:19). When bodily desires dominate, the stomach becomes a god of overconsumption, leading to both spiritual and physical health issues.

Fasting strengthens prayer. In the Bible, fasting is almost always connected to prayer. One time when they were trying to minister deliverance, Jesus told His disciples, "This kind does not go out except by prayer and fasting" (Matthew 17:21 NKJV). Fasting and prayer together bring the greatest results. John Wesley said, "When you seek God with fasting added to prayer, you cannot seek His face in vain."[3] Fasting boosts prayer. Paul ordained new elders with prayer and fasting: "And when they had appointed elders for them in every church, with prayer and fasting they committed them to the Lord in whom they had believed" (Acts 14:23).

Donald Whitney wrote, "Fasting is one of the best friends we can introduce to our prayer life."[4] Prayer connects us to God, and fasting disconnects us from the world. Joel 2:12 says, "Return to me with all your heart, with fasting, with weeping, and with mourning." Fasting helps us turn to God and strengthen our prayer life. Fasting without prayer, while not pointless, will not yield the full power God intends. The purpose of fasting is to strengthen prayer. We disconnect from the world to connect more deeply with God.

Choosing Humility through Fasting

Fasting is a biblical way to humble ourselves. When wicked King Ahab heard the prophet Elijah's rebuke, he tore his clothes, put on sackcloth, and fasted. God noticed Ahab's humility, telling Elijah, "Have you seen how Ahab has humbled himself before me? Because he has humbled himself before me, I will not bring the disaster in his days; but in his son's days I will bring the disaster upon his house" (1 Kings 21:29). David and Ezra also viewed fasting as a means of humility. David said, "I humbled myself with fasting" (Psalm 35:13 NKJV), and Ezra proclaimed a fast "that we might humble ourselves before our God" (Ezra 8:21).

Fasting is a personal expression of humility that gets God's attention. Fasting is not for show or applause. The Bible commands us to humble ourselves before God, not to wait for circumstances to do it. We choose humility by focusing on God and dethroning ourselves through fasting. When fasting is done to humble ourselves before God, it catches His attention. God teaches, lifts up, and gives grace, wisdom, and honor to the humble (see Psalm 25:9; 147:6; Proverbs 3:34; 11:2; 22:4). He dwells with humble people, and they are great in His Kingdom (see Isaiah 57:15; Matthew 18:4). Fasting must be a genuine expression of humility, however, to unlock these promises. Fasting is a powerful companion to prayer and humility.

Fasting openly exposes the unhealthy relationship we can have with food. Food is not your friend! It is meant only to nourish your body. Whenever good food makes people feel happy, they often satisfy their negative emotions or boredom with eating. They call it "comfort food" when excess food becomes a comfort to you. God has promised the Holy Spirit to be our Comforter. The enemy wants us to turn to the fridge for comfort. When you fast, you are forced to deal with these toxic emotions in a new way, by bringing them to the Holy Spirit instead of finding false comfort in food.

Fasting from eating food trains us to share our feelings with the Father instead of with the fridge or pantry. During your fast, not only will physical toxins be removed, but emotional toxins will go as well. Allow the Holy Spirit to cleanse you of soul toxins during the fast. Fasting afflicts and humbles the soul, and weakens its control. You don't need to fast for your spirit, since it is already sealed by the Holy Spirit and made perfect by Jesus' sacrifice. Our spirit is not the problem; it is the soul that's a hindrance. Fasting helps break that soulish barrier in the spirit realm so we can live more spiritual lives.

One Fundamental Principle

The journey to true freedom and spiritual victory hinges on one fundamental principle: *full surrender to Jesus Christ*. Like the boy in the story shared by evangelist Reinhard Bonnke, many of us struggle with giving Jesus complete control over our lives. We often invite Him in, yet we hold back parts of ourselves, thinking we can manage on our own.

It's only when we give Jesus full ownership that we experience true deliverance from our adversaries and challenges. Fasting and prayer play a crucial role in this surrender, disconnecting us from the world and connecting us more deeply with God. Fasting humbles us and strengthens our prayers, drawing us closer to God's heart.

Our deliverance from sin is meant to bring us into a deeper, more committed service to God. True freedom is not just the absence of sin, but the presence of the Holy Spirit filling every part of our lives. The Bible is clear: Jesus is our Savior, but He must also be our Lord. This means acknowledging His ownership over every aspect of our lives, and living in submission to His will. True freedom and spiritual victory come from this complete surrender.

It's not about using God to achieve our goals, but about making Him our ultimate goal. Surrender fully to Him today, and witness the profound changes He will bring.

VLADIMIR SAVCHUK serves as the lead pastor of HungryGen Church, a vibrant multicultural congregation dedicated to soul-winning, healing, deliverance, and the raising up of young leaders. In addition to pastoring, Vladimir extends his ministry through the written word and digital media as an accomplished author, YouTuber, and traveling preacher. He also offers free e-courses through his online learning platform, VladSchool, making theology and Christian living accessible to a global audience.

Vladimir's journey began in Ukraine, where he was born into a devout Christian household. Moving to the United States at the age of thirteen, his calling manifested early when he took on the role of a youth pastor at just sixteen years of age. His dynamic style and deep understanding of Scripture quickly made him a sought-after speaker at various conferences and Christian gatherings. Sharing life and ministry with his wonderful wife, Lana, Vladimir embodies a dynamic approach to leadership and the preaching of God's Word, enriching lives both in his immediate community and well beyond. Pastor Vlad and Lana recently welcomed baby Samuel into the world in March 2024.

8

WORSHIP

JULIE SIGNORELLI

Let the word of Christ dwell in you richly, teaching and admon-
ishing one another in all wisdom, singing psalms and hymns
and spiritual songs, with thankfulness in your hearts to God.

Colossians 3:16

Worship is central and integral to the moves of God
throughout history. Corporate worship has been a
staple of revival. When the people of God come together and
begin to exalt His name above anything and everything, a shift
happens. There is a response God makes when people worship
corporately together.

Yes, God does move in small gatherings. Yes, God does
move in private encounters. But there is a different encounter
that happens when people come together corporately and lift

up praise to the one true living God. God responds with His presence.

I have seen this over and over again in my years of being a believer. I have watched moves of God be questioned, criticized, and rejected by naysayers. I have seen miraculous encounters be categorized as emotional. I have seen the deconstruction community try to discount miraculous manifestations of the Spirit. But the reality is that when you have been a participant in a move of God where you felt His presence, when you have seen real revival, no one can discredit your encounter with God.

Worship Is Necessary for Revival

Worship is necessary for revival. I would be as bold as to say that you cannot have revival without unfiltered corporate worship. Where there are powerful moves of God, you will find powerful worship—worship that touches the heart of God, with God touching the hearts of people in response.

We see time and time again how God moves and responds to corporate gatherings. You cannot separate revival and worship; it's impossible. There cannot be revival without worship.

When we begin worshiping together and put the focus on Jesus, we see the message of Jesus become revelation to those on the outside. Many times, as pastors we hear stories from "outsiders" about how the music opened up their heart. It made them feel something they couldn't quite describe. Then when the message was preached, their heart was postured to receive. This is not emotionalism. This is exactly what the presence of God does in the hearts of men and women. When the focus is put on Him, our hearts become ready to receive Him and to be more like Him.

Some of the greatest songs in church history have come out of revival movements. And yes, I do believe these are great songs in their own right. But I also believe that they carry the oil of a time when God responded to a people putting Him first in a season of worship, dedication, and prayer, worshiping Him first and loving Him first.

Worship Is Demonstrative Revival

I grew up in a Pentecostal church denomination. Worship in our church was demonstrative. I have seen different movements of revival in my short lifetime. Even with movements that have started out more liturgical, as time goes on, people begin responding in a demonstrative way. David responded with dancing. Miriam responded with a tambourine. You see worshipers waving banners and blowing trumpets on the front line of battles in the Old Testament. You see the power of God fall in the New Testament, and none of those things are void of emotion.

The kind of worship that happens in revival is worship from a desperate heart. It is worship that longs for the presence of God to be manifest here on earth. It is worship that longs for the message of Jesus to be important to a generation. It is worship that longs for all idols to be destroyed. It is worship that cannot stay in a "service plan." It goes beyond the thirty-minute allotment for singing. It goes beyond the limits of song. Past the agenda. Revival worship disrupts the norms and schedules of a church. It becomes less about the lyrics. It becomes more about the encounter. And when people encounter the true presence of God, there will be a response.

When you see people praying at the Wailing Wall in Jerusalem, they are demonstrative in their expressions of prayer. When you look further into Jewish culture, their prayers are demonstrative. They are moving, shaking, rocking. They are dancing, yelling, waving. Yet when such expressions have taken place in the Spirit-filled Church, it has been demonized by outsiders and critics of revival, who say that worship should be more liturgical. Although I believe that there is a time and place for liturgical expression, I believe worship should move the heart of God, and it should move your heart out of your comfort zone. You cannot remove the physical demonstrations from revival worship.

The critics of revival will be critical regardless of the demonstrations they observe in worship. It's a demonic critical spirit wanting to keep the Church powerless, voiceless, and bound in conformity. On the outside, I have found some who cry "emotionalism!" Yet critics of the demonstrative worship that expresses emotion have never seen a Jewish celebration. These critics would not attempt to criticize Muslims for their repeated bowing and public praying. They would not criticize Orthodox Jews for rocking while wrapping their arms in the tefillin. But critics of the Spirit-filled churches that are actively moving in revival and demonstrating the Spirit's power are constantly criticizing these churches for the emotionalism they exhibit during worship. It is impossible to separate the two.

Where there is worship, there is the softening of hearts, and there is the dying of self-will. There is trauma that is being dealt with at a deep level. When we are healing in the presence of God, our response can be silence, but it can also be shaking, crying, jumping, running, waving, extravagant giving. This kind of worship and response would have been normal for Jesus to see. And it's always so shocking to me when people try to say that He would be displeased with the forms of worship He sees in church today. If you were to see a Jewish congregation bring a Torah into a synagogue, you would see very quickly that in our spiritual DNA is demonstrative worship. How much more extravagantly should we worship Jesus, the only way to the Father?

Worship Is a Catalyst for Revival

Worship unifies a corporate body. When a room full of people are all singing the same melody and words, it unifies the room in a way only music can. There are so many denominations in the faith. When revival takes place, it has a way of bringing people even in different streams of Christianity together. We see this unity in the time of worship.

I remember hearing about the Brownsville Revival and how there were people coming from every nation. There were churches that gathered from every stream to see what God was doing. My favorite thing when I watch clips back from that revival is to see the diversity in the crowd, and to hear the entire population of that movement singing the same songs while people were touched by the presence of God as He moved so powerfully. When you watch the clips, it really does look as though it's just a local church gathering, but the Brownsville Revival brought so many different people together from all different streams of the Church Body. Worship was the thing that unified every person in the room. A corporate body worshiping with a pure heart in unity touches the heart of God and is a catalyst for revival.

A corporate body worshiping with a pure heart in unity touches the heart of God and is a catalyst for revival.

When I was a very young person watching news coverage of the Brownsville Revival on TV, or seeing clips of it on TBN, the picture would be fuzzy because we didn't have cable. Then we would have to wait for the songs to be recorded and made available for sale at Christian bookstores. When those songs trickled into our church, it felt as if we were part of the revival. It didn't matter that we were in Northwest Indiana six months behind the first time the songs were sung in Florida. The sounds of revival through worship unified us in the movement. The anointing was on the songs from that revival, and you can still feel it today. When I'm in a gathering and we begin to bring back songs from that encounter, you feel the oil from the past reviving hearts in the present.

Worship is a cornerstone for revival. It is not an accident that some of the most powerful songs that we sing today come from times and seasons of revival in the Church. When we sing them today, you can still sense the ember fires of revival.

Revival Worship Is Sincere

The worship in revival cannot be scripted. There's not a formula. Revival worship has to come from a sincere heart that truly wants to see God worshiped as He wants to be worshiped. I see a lot of services labeled "revival." I know what the organizers are trying to say and accomplish. They want to breathe fresh fire into their church or gathering.

One time, I even sat in an office where a gentleman was explaining how additional services add financial margin to a church. We were there for "revival services," and at the end there was a financial goal that was met. The church celebrated, and I do believe the cause was noble. I don't believe there was a malicious heart. But my heart was grieved. I believe revival is so much more. I believe it must start with sincere worship—with no motive.

Growing up in a Pentecostal church, I have seen many moves of God, and I am so grateful for that heritage. It did produce a gift for discerning of spirits. Now when I get into different encounters, I can discern the kind of encounters that are services and the kind of encounters where the heart is revival.

My husband and I did a revival tour a couple of years ago called the Domino Revival, and one of the really important things to me was that our cry for revival was sincere. Every place we went, if the people chose to give to our ministry, that was fine. But our true motive was simply to go into as many places as possible where there had been previous revivals, to see what God could do. There are places where the power of God fell mightily and some churches experienced a renewal. But you cannot manufacture revival, and you cannot manipulate worship in revival.

True revival is a sincere heart with sincere worship. God is responsible for the outcome. If there is an outpouring, it is only because He wills it.

Worship Pulls from Old Wells

Right before God spoke to our family about doing the Domino Revival tour, we had dinner with a ministry friend who encouraged us to go to the old wells of revival. So we went to different locations where there had been revivals, and we decided to come into those spaces once again to worship God and preach the gospel. We saw many people get saved, healed, set free, and have powerful encounters with God in worship.

The year the Lord gave the vision to my husband about the Domino Revival, I preached a message talking about wells at a women's conference. I didn't realize that the Lord was preparing my heart for the word that a friend gave us just a few months later. We began to meditate on the concept of wells and what it meant. Many times in the Old Testament, you see that wells were stopped up by opposing armies. And you see people digging new wells. Isaac dug a lot of wells:

> And Isaac dug again the wells of water which they had dug in the days of Abraham his father, for the Philistines had stopped them up after the death of Abraham. He called them by the names which his father had called them.
>
> Also Isaac's servants dug in the valley, and found a well of running water there. But the herdsmen of Gerar quarreled with Isaac's herdsmen, saying, "The water is ours." So he called the name of the well Esek, because they quarreled with him. Then they dug another well, and they quarreled over that one also. So he called its name Sitnah. And he moved from there and dug another well, and they did not quarrel over it. So he called its name Rehoboth, because he said, "For now the LORD has made room for us, and we shall be fruitful in the land."
>
> Then he went up from there to Beersheba. And the LORD appeared to him the same night and said, "I am the God of your father Abraham; do not fear, for I am with you. I will bless you and multiply your descendants for My servant Abraham's sake." So he built an altar there and called on the name of the LORD, and he pitched his tent there; and there Isaac's servants dug a well.
>
> Genesis 26:18–25 NKJV

Wells represented the ability to have life. A well was a water source that could satiate an entire community. Wells represented ownership and were used as landmarks. Wells also represented places where people had encountered God and marked His provision.

Brownsville is a well of revival. Azuza Street is a well of revival. There are places of miraculous encounters that have been marked by God. These are supernatural. They cannot be engineered, and they cannot be socially motivated. It is impossible to bring that many people into unity for that long without the supernatural hand of God allowing it.

There is something about the worship that comes from those wells. A lot of the songs were spontaneous choruses that were sung in times of impartation and inspiration. When we sing them today, we are remembering what God did before and what He will do again. If God had revival in one season, He will have it again. And worship is the celebration of renewal—celebrating what God has done and celebrating what God will do again.

Worship Is Supernatural

You cannot separate the supernatural from revival worship. Revival cannot even be the goal when true revival worship breaks forth. Worship has to be purehearted. No motive. The only motive is to lift the name of Jesus high, yield to God, and sacrifice whatever He is asking of you in that moment. When worship is pure, God responds with His presence.

I have had two tangible supernatural, miraculous encounters during worship. When Michael and I were youth pastors in our twenties, we were in a youth service where we began to worship God. Our band was not that skilled. But we began to worship, and we began to sing phrases over and over and over. When I opened my eyes, I saw a mist in the room, and I thought that we had turned on a machine of some sort. Or I thought maybe there was an issue in the room. And my flesh

Worship has to be purehearted. No motive. The only motive is to lift the name of Jesus high, yield to God, and sacrifice whatever He is asking of you in that moment.

---

was trying to comprehend that this surely must be something unusual going on with my eyes. Finally, I leaned over to Mike and said, "Do you see this?"

And he said, "Jules, we are in the Glory."

I couldn't believe it. We were seeing God's presence in a tangible way. God's presence was physically in the room. We didn't ask for such an encounter. In fact, we were young professionals raising a baby. It was a weeknight, and we were very tired. However, there was something about when we pushed the program of our service aside and focused on honoring the Lord. We saw the tangible presence of God come into the room.

I remember being filled with such hope, and I have gone back to that moment many times. Since then, I have taken classes on church planting. I have been to many conferences and read many books. I have examined commentary critical of being driven by emotionalism, to make sure that I haven't fallen victim to it. I want to be of sound doctrine. I want to be wise. I want to be respected in my field as someone who is both supernatural and intellectual. But I go back to that moment often, and I remember how everything about that moment would have been criticized by many who were on the outside, looking in. There were kids shaking, crying, and praying in tongues. There was not a ton of organization, or a service plan of where we were going next. We were just simply doing the Pentecostal thing of repeating a phrase over and over. When we got to a certain point, it was as though a well had been dug up and the presence of God was released.

I don't think we deserved it. I certainly don't believe we were looking for it. I didn't even know you could ask for such an encounter. But in God's merciful way, He showed up. Worship is supernatural, and you cannot separate supernatural worship from revival.

The other encounter I had was when I attended junior camp as a child. All the churches in our state within our denomination hosted a junior camp and senior camp every year. And every year, God met the campers in a powerful way. I would say I was more of an observer in those times, not necessarily a full participant, as my personality was always more reserved.

Every year at camp, they hosted one service where the junior and senior camps combined. One year at this combined service, we began to sing a song about possessing the land. People were marching around for hours and hours, and it was definitely a picture of something that probably would get made fun of on the internet. There were people who were running, shaking, and flailing around. People began to go outside and worship. Everyone was singing the same phrase over and over. And at some juncture, someone exclaimed, "There's an angel outside!"

When I went outside, there was a ten-foot glowing angel in a tree. I could see every detail of the angel's face with my physical eyes. I want to reiterate: This was something we all saw with our physical eyes. This was not in our spiritual hearts. I saw the wind blowing the angel's hair, and the angel's garments were flowing. There was a sash with a long item that looked as if it was a sword. The angel stayed in that tree for over an hour. I could not believe what I was seeing. I kept rubbing my eyes and squinting. And people were absolutely overcome with emotion. To this day, I still cannot fathom what I saw and experienced in that service.

Today, many churches, especially in my country of America, would not be patient enough to go past the limits of a service into the kind of worship that led us to that encounter. I can't think of one place where the kind of demonstrative worship that

I saw that day at camp would be welcomed. I'm so grateful for the leaders in that church camp, who allowed God space and time to move. I'm not sure why, but the Lord sent an angel that day. I know you might be reading this and not believe it, but there were over one hundred kids who saw what I saw that day. It forever changed the way I thought about worship and encountering God.

Again, you cannot separate the supernatural from revival worship. If you worship long enough, God's presence will manifest itself in some way. That day at camp, it was a physical manifestation of an angel. A decade later, it was the physical manifestation of a mist or a glory cloud that showed up in that youth group service in Portage, Indiana. We have had services where we've been singing and people have gotten healed and set free immediately. They've been supernaturally freed of things that would take years for medication, therapy, or addiction recovery to help them progress in. God was able to do it in moments in a worship service. I don't know why God moves the way He does, or why He responds the way He does, but corporate worship attracts the presence of God in a supernatural way.

JULIE SIGNORELLI cofounded V1 Church alongside her husband, Mike. She serves as the director of V1 Community Impact, where she oversees food pantry operations in NYC and Northwest Indiana and coordinates Christmas gift programs for families in NYC. She is the global worship pastor for V1 Worship, which recently signed with Dream Records, and founded the Free Women Collective, a thriving women's ministry reaching women all over the world. When not leading revival movements or homeschooling her daughters Everly and Bella, Julie can be found enjoying brunch and shopping.

9

THE COMING FAMILY REVIVAL

> In that day I will raise up the booth of David that is fallen and repair its breaches, and raise up its ruins and rebuild it as in the days of old.
>
> Amos 9:11

During our first year of ministry, we made a decision together that we wouldn't sacrifice family for ministry, but at every tension point we would always sacrifice ministry for family instead. Now, I'll be honest—it hasn't been the easiest thing to do in the world of westernized ministry, and it has been the priciest of paths, the most unpopular, and one we have had to grow thick skin to endure as we have pioneered. But it's a hill that we decided long ago to die upon, because the alternative is far worse. So to the other pioneers of family out there, or to those already intrigued and longing to see greater health in the Church, this chapter is for you.

Right now, I can't help but think of Martin Luther. I always imagined that the moment he sat down to pen the 95 Theses, he was overcome by the Spirit to the point that he no longer thought about the fear of man, his own life, his career, or anything else. He was burning with zeal and a message of reformation for the Church that would change her trajectory so massively that it would alter the course of history. It's with that same zeal and weighty overshadowing that I sit here, prepared to be the pen of a ready writer, and with a similar reformational message from God's heart that will shift the course of the Church and lead her into her best days.

Before I begin, I want to preface what I have to say by laying this foundational statement and plea to the Church: The vehicle of this next move of God must be the vehicle of family. How can we adequately reveal the heart of the Father to a hurting world without family? It would be like a speech without a translator in a foreign nation. It wouldn't connect. We can't go another inch without it. It has become my life's mission to walk this path and invite others into the revival that is in its infancy—the revival of family.

Back to the Garden

I once heard it said that the gospel is the story of a Father who lost His kids in the garden, and because He couldn't bear to live without them, He "bankrupted heaven" to get them back. I remember the day that I heard this, because I was on a journey from spiritual orphan to sonship with God, and the impact of this simple quote revolutionized me profoundly.

My whole life, I had not seen God as a Father, but more as a Master, Boss, or Godfather. I understood those roles, because I thought that as long as I worked hard and performed my religious duties, I was good with Him. That fit my grade A, people-pleaser mentality perfectly. But a Father? Really? I knew that technically He was a Father, but experientially, no. He was someone I submitted to, gave my religious worship to on Sunday, paid my tithes to, and prayed to when I felt like it. That, I understood. In a church setting, it only made sense that I submitted to His managers or pastors. I attended regularly and didn't miss a service unless I was dying. I served as many days and nights as I could, and in return, I felt like a good Christian. That's Christianity, right? So this one saying about God bankrupting heaven for me started to wreck me in the worst and best of ways, but it was only the beginning of what was to come.

It's safe to say that we've all been in environments where pastors and leaders were more like CEOs than like fathers or leaders. This must have been an issue even in the time of the early Church, that humanity was constantly trying to become an organized religion over a family. In this hour, I believe the Lord is bringing us back to His original design and intent. He is breaking the CEO-model of the Church and the hierarchy, and He is bringing us back to our truest and most secure foundation for the days to come.

But, let me back it up and share a little of my story.

Born into Dysfunction

I grew up in a place called Redcliffe, Australia—the same place the Bee Gees grew up in, which is ironic considering that they were the picture of a tight-knit, supportive, and loving family. My experience was a little different.

I was four years old when my dad left my mother, my brother, and me. During that time, I remember that my mum cried a lot, and I wrestled with the thought that his leaving was my fault. I also remember the few years after that being tough. My mum worked a few jobs to keep the mortgage paid and food on the table.

When I was six, my mum remarried. It didn't take long to discover that this man was not what he seemed. All I knew of family from then on were fights and chaos. There were countless family feuds and family reunions that ended in drunken, violent fights as we kids watched on through the boards in the stairs.

Without knowing any better, I just knew that this couldn't be normal. Something in me began to ache and long for a healthy environment, a safe place where I could be myself and be loved, whatever that looked like. But as I looked around at church, at other families, and at my friends in my neighborhood, I realized that family chaos was far from unusual. For the people I knew, at least, pain, brokenness, and dysfunction were the norm.

So why was I longing for something healthy? I realize now that it was my spirit telling me that there was more. And besides that, my orphan heart was craving the love of my heavenly Father.

Have We Sold Our Birthright?

I often wonder, *Has the Church sold its birthright?*

Like Esau, who in a moment of weakness gave over what was valuable for a bowl of soup (see Genesis 25:29–34), has the Church given over its birthright for something that doesn't even compare?

We can all look at big buildings, mega-hierarchies, and perfectly administrated movements and marvel at them. But like a mansion without a family to make it a home, what is it? The vacuum that family is meant to occupy is a recipe for disaster as something else sneakily creeps in and takes up residence. Institution inserts itself, or as I like to call it, the organized orphanage—a place where people come together under the banner of their faith, but without the foundation of family. This looks and sounds good, but under the surface it is a ticking time bomb in families, marriages, and communities.

After years of serving in ministries around the world, traveling on the road full-time as a married couple, and serving in local churches, my wife and I felt as if something was missing, but we couldn't quite put our finger on what it was. For us, it came down to one season when we were helping with a new church plan. We loved the vision, and the people were amazing, but the time commitment was grueling. It meant that I had to be at church early on a Sunday, while Christy had to get the girls ready and drive quite a distance herself three out of four Sundays. On my Sundays off, we fought all the way to church, until we walked in the door pretending it was all sunshine and roses.

One particular Sunday, after spending a week with Christy's grandfather who was dying of cancer, we arrived at church late. As we entered the door, the pastor was asking this question: "Where are the committed ones who will give up everything to be in the house of God? Where are the ones who will put their vision, families, and needs after building the house?"

Christy looked at me with a look I had never seen before. It was the look of someone who had just found the last straw. "That's not the Kingdom we are building!" she said.

And I couldn't have agreed more. Safe to say, we decided to pull back and prioritize family from that moment on. We had been sucked back into the machine without realizing it, but now were fully aware of how seductive and charming it can be when this kind of culture that feeds and coddles your self-worth is all we have known. Only a year after this, we stepped into full-time ministry as a family.

Getting to the Root

Before I say what comes next, you need to know my heart. I'm not anti-church. I attend a church, I have many pastor friends, and I love the local church. Yet I'm grateful to be able to be part of the current expression, surrounded by people like me who are always pressing forward or "pioneering" toward where God is leading the Church today. The only thing I am against is the enemy's agenda to weaken, dilute, divert, stifle, muzzle, or lead the Church away from who she is meant to be. My beef isn't with leaders or people; it's with the spirit of this age, which is knocking at the door to sell some compromises. Unfortunately, many have taken the bait, and these compromises always rob the family.

Some years ago, shortly before a well-known pastor was exposed for a moral failure and mismanagement of his staff, I had a dream. In the dream, my friend who was involved in the movement invited me to swim in the pool at a penthouse. As I got in, I saw his eyes grow wide, as if he was worried that I was about to discover something. Sure enough, I felt something sticky on my feet, so I got out and discerned that it was bird feces. I asked God, *What is this?*

The Lord responded, *There is an unclean spirit that has been allowed here, and no one is addressing it!*

Then sure enough, it played out in real life the way I had seen in the dream. These compromises always affect families, and that's devastating to me. I have watched over the years as this has happened over and over in many different ministries. Why does it happen this way? Because we have elevated ministries above families, yes, but also above our relationship with God. We have made a golden calf of the institution, and many don't know how to let go when it matters. As a byproduct of this, people in ministry unfortunately lose their marriages and families.

So, what's the root? It's too easy to say the spirit of religion, even though that's part of the recipe. I want to suggest that the culprit is none other than the queen of counterfeits, Jezebel herself. The name *Jezebel* means unhusbanded, so this spirit will attach itself to anything pure and slowly make it a *de facto* expression of what it once was or was meant to be.

The Jezebel spirit can't stand true connection or an environment where the Holy Spirit has free rein. She will do anything she can to get on the inside and twist the vision and agenda of a ministry until it begins to grow different fruit than God originally designed. She does this by inflating people's egos and flattering them through grand opportunities and grand-scale ideas that seem right, but have a huge cost in the long run. Not that things of magnitude are not of God. I'm just stating that one of this spirit's tactics is to blindside leaders with their ambition and their love of their own reputation.

This is also the same stronghold that leads prophets and apostles astray. Jezebel hates the family, and that's why families have struggled for a long time under the current regime. But it's changing!

The Wrong Fathering Movement

A few months ago, I was walking through our house and praying over one of our family members who was struggling with identity issues when I heard the Lord say, *Woe to the wrong father!*

Then out of my spirit, I began to prophesy, declaring,

> Where the Church has been absent as fathers to this generation, false fathers have crept in and are raising and grooming them in lies and twisted identity. But now we will see a new fathering and mothering movement arise that will *flip the script* on this current movement that is blinding their hearts and minds.

We won't let this demonic agenda and giant continue to go unchallenged. We will take down this Philistine with the blood of the Lamb and our voices and testimonies. We will see captives set free to become our generation's greatest harvest!

It's time for the fathers and mothers to arise and speak truth, coupled with the baptism of love and true identity.

The Age of Empires Is Over

The age of empires is over, and the era of family is here again. Somehow, family has gotten lost since the days of Acts. Somewhere along the way, we traded true fellowship for the mission. The mission is important, but it doesn't replace the power of what is birthed through authentic community. It's both together. In the wake of this loss, a monster has arisen—a schism, a Frankenstein of epic religious proportions. Suddenly, brick and mortar are the idol, the building is the great prize, and filling it is the only objective.

People's bums on seats and money in the bucket. Is that really what God wants? Weren't we the Church Jesus died for? Weren't we the Bride, or did that change hands along the way and usher in the age of institutions and mega-corporations?

We got fired, and the LLC era arrived. Franchises entered the scene, and religious brands filled the earth with their marketing angles and sales pitches. In the void of anything resembling real connection, the age of empires thrived. Beggars can't be choosers, right? "Open the doors, sign on the dotted line, let us tell you what God is saying, and let us use you to build our thing."

It looked good, and it felt great to be needed, but then came the day when we realized that the bricks were sand and the foundations were a swamp of dysfunction and tragic error. We woke up one day and realized that we were pouring ourselves out unnecessarily. We began to wonder, *What have we done to ourselves?*

We weren't any more connected to God or people. We were disconnected from God, placing our serving before our relationships and our allegiance to the leaders before our responsibility to Almighty God. We lost our fear of the Lord. Our reverence and our spiritual compass were off-center. We were more isolated than when we began. We came for guidance and to belong, and we were now even farther from the shore—except now we were also empty, burned out, and disillusioned. What happened? We built empires when we were designed to build a *family*.

We wanted a covering so badly that we didn't realize that what we were desiring was a covenant. Covering was meant to bring freedom, but it brought bondage and control. It was meant to bring alignment and peace, but it brought demonic soul ties and muzzling. We signed the contract and were suffering from its fine print. We were deceived that we were in union with God, but instead we were in bed with the spirit of religion and man's conquest. We were the casualties of war, again. Yes, again. Around the mountain we had gone again, in hopes that this time it would be different. But we fell into the same trap.

I'm saying this to you because we were designed to build a different house altogether. The house we were called to build was family. It's people, it's the Body of Christ, it's humanity! "For we are God's fellow workers. You are God's field, God's building" (1 Corinthians 3:9).

So, what are you pioneering? What are you building? The old house or the new?

Jesus told some Jews who were questioning His methods, "Destroy this temple, and in three days I will raise it up" (John 2:19). What if I were to say that you were called to tear down the old and rebuild the new? Does that mean we dishonor the old? No, but in building the new, we must oppose and expose the schism that produced the whitewashed tombs of the Pharisees.

The Call to Build Legacy

If you are one of the pioneers building legacy right now over building empires, few will recognize or see what you are building, because it's an underground mission. It's a call to build low and slow, while the rest of the ministry world is building fast and publicly. It's a calling that takes place behind the stage and often doesn't look glamorous. It's the call to build the family over the organization. It's moving away from the hustle, and building what is organic and homegrown. It's the call to establish deep roots that extend beyond your lifetime, and build a future for future generations.

It's a call to address generational strongholds, cycles, and injustices, and to break demonic bloodlines, to establish healthy ones. It's the call to set new foundations and prioritize health and wholeness over public image and reputation. It's the call to reverse the messes of the religious institution that built empires at the cost of leaving orphans in its wake. It's the call to forfeit the plans and goals that produce immediate results, for the building and pioneering of what takes many years to show above the surface.

Many are in the tension of this call because they no longer feel the pull of the conference circuit or the appetite for a lifestyle they once valued. It may feel as though you are going in reverse or have lost your favor, but this couldn't be further from the truth. The Father has thrown His mantle around your shoulders, and you have begun to burn the old plow and start on this new path. If this is you, then you need to know today that you are not lazy, rebellious, in error, or strange for feeling this call. This is the call of *spiritual* mothers and fathers to establish the family, set the table, and call in the lonely and lost. It's the call to focus on the health of what you are building over prioritizing its stature.

What is the point of building something big if it's unhealthy or compromised? What good is building a sandcastle in the sand? Even if it looks magnificent today, it's going to be washed away tomorrow.

Breaking Generational Cycles

God is after your foundation. This is the call to raise your family well, pioneer even healthier marriages, discover God's design in covenant relationships and in the house of Acts community, and raise a generation that knows how to represent the Kingdom well. In a time where the anti-family culture of the world has begun to invade the Church, God has called many to the front lines to rebuild and reset the definition and design of God's house so we can be a force to be reckoned with.

So, let me say it again: The days of building empires are over! There is no more juice left in that wineskin. The grace period to keep prioritizing brick and mortar over sons and daughters is over. The heart of God is brooding over family, and if you are looking for what God's pulse is on right now, that's it. Not a fake family. Not a plastic, inauthentic, religious cliché family, but real family. We have been so good at building structures, administratively creating perfect organizations and systems, and managing people that we have lost the very heart of the Father. If you are wondering what to build, build a family and repair it. Champion the family. Fight for the family. That's why the enemy is warring so hard after the family and the values of the Kingdom family, because he sees that family is the future.

If you are wondering what to build, build a family and repair it. Champion the family. Fight for the family.

The enemy sees that family is the key that unlocks harvest and an army of uncompromising burning ones. The tide of culture is warring against the family right now, but we get to be the wave that pushes it back. The days of the enemy tearing down our homes are over. It's been an injustice, and one that God is correcting. That's why religion can't be our idol, nor ministry our mistress. We have to protect the home. We can't be lovers of the boardroom more than the family room. We can't keep sacrificing our children on the altar of "doing Kingdom." We can't keep letting Disney raise our kids while we are off doing fire tunnels. We can't keep letting Netflix and computer games numb our kids to the reality of the Spirit. We must build the altar in the home again. We have to lead our families into the presence and a real encounter.

This is a "change of gears" season when God is anchoring us back to what matters. That's why you've been feeling an internal shift of priorities, and why your appetite has changed.

That's God showing you where He wants you to move. It's a season of stepping into a different flow, off the hamster wheel and into the slipstream of the Spirit. It's a season of less is more, and you will be so surprised by what God produces when your eyes are set to less. With Him, the less becomes more.

It's a season of taking back the family mountain for the Kingdom, stripping false kings of their titles and evicting them from their thrones. It's a season of finally coming into stability and an establishment for families who have been in the long hallway of transition for many years. God is planting you to make you into a pillar, the shade, and a refuge for so many others. This is the birthplace of revival, and this is what the pioneering was all for.

It's About to Get Messy

This is the season when we are moving away from the manicured to the messy, from ducks in a row to being utterly reliant on the Spirit. But the fruit will speak for itself. Empires have successfully created clones and obedient servants but have failed to raise friends of God who know His voice.

Family is restoring everything that religion has defiled. We are on a take-back mission, and the lost are coming home. The isolated and those camped out on the fringe, rejected and outcast, those who don't fit the criteria of the system, are coming home. The table is being spread, and the prodigals are already beginning to run. We must be ready with a ring and a robe.

It's that time. God is getting you ready. Right now, He is severing all unhealthy attachments and ties to you. He is setting the record straight over your home. The generational dysfunctions you grew up in are no longer yours to continue. This is a season when God begins a new thing in your home. Kingdom legacy is beginning. He has started a new bloodline that begins with you right now, at this moment. I prophesy this:

Legacy begins here and now. This is where it changes. Our kids will not grow up tormented, demonized, gender confused, addicted, or unsure of who they are. They will be sons and daughters of God who know their identity and purpose, pursuers of God's heart, and restorers of those who are broken. Our marriages will no longer be attacked, assassinated, broken down, and destroyed. Our marriages will be holy and set apart. Not like the world's ways, but built upon the rock—in Jesus' name!

The Spirit of Adoption

In 2020, Christy and I joined Sean Feucht on the Golden Gate Bridge in San Francisco for what would be his first public prayer-and-worship event during the COVID-19 lockdown. As we were worshiping together, suddenly I stepped into a vision where I saw the arms of the Father reaching out over the city, and with tears in His eyes, He was seeking after the hearts of those who were hurting and living in sin, addiction, and bondage. Then I began to prophesy, "The spirit of adoption is here! The spirit of adoption is here! Won't you respond?"

I was in travail for weeks after that day, feeling the abandonment and trauma of a fatherless generation who simply didn't know that a Father was wanting to take them in and heal their wounds. It got to the point where I was feeling such anguish over it that I didn't know what to do. Then the Lord said to me, *Father them.*

Paul said in 1 Corinthians 4:15, "For though you have countless guides in Christ, you do not have many fathers. For I became your father in Christ Jesus through the gospel." I believe this passage was hinting at the fact that even in the days of the early Church, there was a strong rise of knowledgeable people on their soapboxes but a massive deficit of spiritual mothers and fathers. What's the difference? Teachers impart what you do, but mothers and fathers impart who you are. They instill legacy and inheritance and responsibility, rather than just submission, servanthood, and unfortunately control. This is why we need the "spirit of adoption" days to begin and the days of the orphanage to come to an end.

Let me break it down deeper for you. For much of history, the Church has been viewed primarily as an institution—a structured organization with hierarchies, programs, and methods. The institutional model has its strengths, providing order and stability. There has been a growing realization, however, that this approach can sometimes overshadow true connection, fellowship, and family.

The spirit of adoption, from a corporate view, calls believers into a deep, familial relationship with God and with each other. Jesus' teachings and the writings of the apostles consistently use familial language to describe the community of believers. Paul in particular emphasizes this in Romans 8 and Galatians 4. He speaks of the spirit of adoption enabling believers to call God "Abba, Father." Romans 8:14–17 reveals the weighty truth that outside of being fathered by God, we are slaves to a system or a false kingdom:

> For all who are led by the Spirit of God are sons of God. For you did not receive the spirit of slavery to fall back into fear, but you have received the Spirit of adoption as sons, by whom we cry, "Abba! Father!" The Spirit himself bears witness with our spirit that we are children of God, and if children, then

heirs—heirs of God and fellow heirs with Christ, provided we suffer with him in order that we may also be glorified with him.

Wow! And Galatians 4:4–7 goes even deeper, to reveal how Jesus set us free from the law and illegitimacy, and made us heirs, and sons and daughters:

> But when the fullness of time had come, God sent forth his Son, born of woman, born under the law, to redeem those who were under the law, so that we might receive adoption as sons. And because you are sons, God has sent the Spirit of his Son into our hearts, crying, "Abba! Father!" So you are no longer a slave, but a son, and if a son, then an heir through God.

These passages highlight that through the Holy Spirit, we are adopted into God's family, and this should radically transform the way we view our relationship with Him and with each other. This adoption means that we are not members of an organization, but are children, part of a family!

Returning to Acts

If we look at the period when Jesus was alive, we see the tension of these same two systems. The first was the religious system of the Pharisees, and the second was what Jesus was introducing. These two systems clash on multiple levels. But why?

As in Jesus' day, I have people say to me all the time, "But, Nate, we need the structure and the protocols." I'm not against the structure. I can see the strengths of the institution, such as:

- Widespread reach
- Consistency

- Strong administration
- Order and stability

But what also comes with the institution has been:

- Control and forced submission
- Hierarchies, clichés, and elitism
- Rigidity and boxing in the Holy Spirit
- Organization over family
- Program-driven over Spirit-led

What are the missing elements? The lack of freedom of the Spirit, and the Father heart of God.

I want to propose that you can have the strengths of the structure, as well as have family thriving within a framework of sorts that still allows for the Holy Spirit to do what He wants. I'd say it like this: In the same way that the mind is a great servant but a lousy master, when we put systems in place as servants to the movement of the Spirit, it works—but not the other way around. When family becomes the foundation again, we will find that we aren't throwing the baby out with the bath water, just throwing out the stuff that keeps blocking the pipe. We have to get back to the book of Acts again!

> And they devoted themselves to the apostles' teaching and the fellowship, to the breaking of bread and the prayers. And awe came upon every soul, and many wonders and signs were being done through the apostles. And all who believed were together and had all things in common. And they were selling their possessions and belongings and distributing the proceeds to all, as any had need. And day by day, attending the temple together

and breaking bread in their homes, they received their food with glad and generous hearts, praising God and having favor with all the people. And the Lord added to their number day by day those who were being saved.

Acts 2:42–47

Can you see the shift in the passage above? What does that look like in today's world?

The spirit of adoption calls for the Church to move beyond the confines of institutionalism and embrace its true identity as a family. This transformation involves prioritizing relationships, fostering shared leadership, encouraging organic growth, and providing holistic care. As churches rediscover these foundational principles, they can become vibrant, loving communities that reflect the heart of God in a way we are only beginning to see emerge. In doing so, the Church not only honors its biblical heritage, but also becomes a compelling witness to the world. In a society often marked by isolation and fragmentation, a Church that lives as a genuine family offers a powerful alternative—a place of belonging, love, and hope.

The Family and Army

Many years ago, I was studying the word *ecclesia* when I heard Dutch Sheets speak about a concept I had never found before. He talked about the Greek word *oikos* in the New Testament and how we as the Church are meant to be both the *oikos* and the *ecclesia*.[1]

Oikos means household or family, while *ecclesia* refers to an assembly or gathering. Together, they paint a picture of the Church as both a nurturing family and a mobilized army, ready to impact the world. In the New Testament, the idea of *oikos* is central to how the early Christians saw themselves. They were more than just members of a religious group; they were family. In Ephesians 2:19, Paul writes, "So then you are no longer strangers and aliens, but you are fellow citizens with the saints and members of the household of God."

In an *oikos* model, relationships are foremost. Church members see each other as brothers and sisters, investing time and effort into building genuine connections. An *oikos* church takes care of its members in every aspect—spiritually, emotionally, and practically. This means praying for each other, offering counseling, helping out with practical needs, and just being there for one another. Church is no longer just about Sunday services. It's about doing life together throughout the week—whether that's in small groups, home gatherings, or community activities. This way, faith becomes part of everyday life, not just something for the weekends.

The term *ecclesia* originally referred to a civic assembly, often gathered for important decisions or military action. In the New Testament, it describes the Church as a purposeful, mission-driven community. In Matthew 16:18, Jesus says, "And I tell you, you are Peter, and on this rock I will build my church, and the gates of hell shall not prevail against it." In 2 Timothy 2:3, Paul says, "Share in suffering as a good soldier of Christ Jesus."

An *ecclesia* church has a clear sense of mission. Members see themselves as part of God's army, called to spread the gospel and serve their communities. This involves outreach, social justice, and making a real difference in the world. The *ecclesia* model recognizes that there's a spiritual battle going on. Churches emphasize prayer, spiritual disciplines, and equipping believers to stand firm against challenges and opposition. An *ecclesia* church is always ready to mobilize its members for service. This might mean training and sending people out on missions, or organizing local outreach efforts. Everyone has a role to play, and the church operates like a coordinated team.

I believe that where we are going, we need a convergence of both *oikos* and *ecclesia*. It's a place where deep, supportive relationships thrive, but also where there's a strong sense of mission and purpose. By fostering an *oikos* environment, a church ensures that members are cared for and connected. This creates a strong foundation where people feel loved and supported. At the same time, embracing the *ecclesia* model keeps a church outward focused. Members are equipped and sent out to impact the world in various ways. This convergence allows a church to be both a loving family and a powerful force for change.

By prioritizing relationships and embracing mission, the Church becomes a place where people can truly belong and make a difference. In a world that often feels disconnected and purposeless, the Church as *oikos* and *ecclesia* is a community where every member is valued, supported, and mobilized for a greater purpose. This is the Church Jesus envisioned—a family on a mission, united in love and purpose.

Pioneering Family Amidst Toxic Culture

Pioneering family in the context of our own personal family has been the greatest joy and yet the hardest road, all in one. Most people don't get it. I can't even tell you how many invites Christy and I have received from ministries wanting to host us, but requesting that our kids don't come to the meeting. We decided long ago to say yes to far fewer invites and focus on partnering with ministries that saw us as a family. This became our rule of thumb: If the door is big enough for our whole family to walk through, then we will. That never meant we expected ministries to pay for our kids; we always did that. But it was the courtesy of respecting that, for us, our family wasn't the side thing, but the main thing!

So, our girls have been traveling with us since Charlotte was four years old and Sophie was two. They are pros on the long-haul flights now! Ava was born in the United States and started traveling when she was three months old. We do it all together, and that's just how we roll.

This became our rule of thumb: If the door is big enough for our whole family to walk through, then we will.

What people don't understand is that we don't do this for convenience, because trust me, it's not. But it's essential. We do this because of the battle we have chosen. We didn't come to America to build a ministry, but something completely different. We lived in the United States in 2009 and 2010, and it was shortly after returning to Australia in 2011 that the Lord said that we were going to be sent back to take down the giant of Roe v. Wade. That was a huge part of our mission here. Now we are called to chase out the rest of his brothers!

Pioneering families amidst toxic culture can feel like constant opposition, but it's also the very reason we have to do it. The enemy is raging hard against our kids and rapidly increasing his propaganda and ideologies in the earth, but the answer is here—families not sheltered from the mess and evil, but active and engaged within. That's the very core of why it's important for families to rise up and be a voice in these times.

In the Rebuilding

As I begin to wind up this chapter, I feel like Nehemiah coming before the king:

I said to the king, "May the king live forever! Why should my face not look sad, when the city where my ancestors are buried lies in ruins, and its gates have been destroyed by fire?"

Then the king said to me, "What is it you want?"

Then I prayed to the God of heaven, and I answered the king, "If it pleases the king and if your servant has found favor in his sight, let him send me to the city in Judah where my ancestors are buried so that I can rebuild it."

Nehemiah 2:3–5 NIV

Or Esther coming before the king in Esther 5:3 (NIV): "Then the king asked, 'What is it, Queen Esther? What is your request? Even up to half the kingdom, it will be given to you.'"

And I feel the charge in this apostolic letter to you is the same. I pray it not only grips you, but also overtakes your life, as it has for me. The walls of the home must be rebuilt! We are on a rescue mission to take back the family of God from the enemy, where he has been trying to rob marriages, steal our kids' identities, and kill our children in the womb. Just as these passages from Nehemiah 4:14 and Esther 4:14 converge:

Don't be afraid. . . . Remember the LORD, who is great and awesome, and fight for your families, your sons and your daughters, your wives and your homes.

Nehemiah 4:14 NIV

For if you keep silent at this time, relief and deliverance will rise for the Jews from another place, but you and your father's house will perish. And who knows whether you have not come to the kingdom for such a time as this?

Esther 4:14

154

The charge for you is this: *You can't be silent.*

In the last three hundred years, we have seen the Great Awakening (1730s–1740s), the Second Great Awakening (early nineteenth century), the Welsh Revival (1904–1905), the Azusa Street Revival (1906–1915), the Korean Revival (1907), the Hebrides Revival (1949–1952), the East African Revival (1920s–1970s), the Jesus Movement (late 1960s–early 1970s), the Brownsville Revival (1995–2000), the Toronto Blessing (1994–present), and in the last fifteen years what I like to call the "awakening of the remnant." But what if what's to come is the great family revival? The awakening of the Church to spiritual arms for the current generation lost in the swirl of identity deception, the seduction of a Jezebel culture, the devaluing of life in the womb, the breakdown of biblical female and male roles, and the perversion of the marriage covenant? What if this next revival is going to rescue people out of the prisons of religious institutional bondage and reveal the Father's heart of God and the spirit of adoption to a Church and a world that haven't known Him?

Revealing Jesus through Family

A few years ago, our girls became good friends with a neighbor child. We knew the family wasn't Christian, and that grieved Charlotte so much that she prayed for them all day long: "Lord, show them who You are!"

Then one night, Charlotte had a dream where she saw a demonic spirit entering this family's house and creating bad dreams. She woke up and prayed for them. The next day, she asked them about having bad dreams, and one of the parents gasped because a child was indeed being tormented at night with such dreams. They had even tried having someone come over and perform an occult cleansing ritual in their house, to chase the demons out.

When Charlotte heard this, she very matter-of-factly told them, "Well, that does nothing, but you probably invited some more demons in!"

They then asked Charlotte what she thought they should do. She asked if she and I could come over to their house and pray, and they said yes, so we did. No more bad dreams!

But that wasn't Charlotte's goal. She wanted them saved. One day a week later, as our girls were playing with their friend, I felt the anointing strong in our house. I walked around the corner to hear Charlotte preaching to this child, who responded with tears running down both cheeks. Moments later, Charlotte led this friend to Jesus!

> But we have this treasure in jars of clay, to show that the surpassing power belongs to God and not to us. We are afflicted in every way, but not crushed; perplexed, but not driven to despair; persecuted, but not forsaken; struck down, but not destroyed; always carrying in the body the death of Jesus, so that the life of Jesus may also be manifested in our bodies.
>
> 2 Corinthians 4:7–10

The great last days' revealing of Jesus—*apocalypto*—will keep happening through stadiums and massive outreach events.[2] But let's not forget the secret weapon that the enemy thought would be a no contest: God wants to reveal Himself through family.

NATE JOHNSTON is an Australian prophetic voice, author, and revivalist passionate about awakening people to their identity and calling in Christ. Known for championing the "wild ones" and pioneering voices, Nate calls the church to break free from religious mindsets and embrace intimacy with God. Alongside his wife, Christy, he leads Everyday Revivalists, equipping believers to walk in bold faith and uncompromised truth, and RMNT, a training platform for emerging voices. Nate's ministry invites people into transformation, empowering them to bring revival and reformation to their communities. Nate and Christy live with their three daughters in Colorado Springs, Colorado.

10

PENTECOST: PERPETUAL REVIVAL

MIKE SIGNORELLI

The city of Jerusalem was buzzing with activity. It was almost time for the Passover feast, and everyone was getting ready. This was when the special Passover lamb had to be sacrificed. Now, this wasn't just any ordinary lamb. It held a deep meaning for the people. You see, the lamb was sacrificed because of people's mistakes and wrongdoings. It was as if the lamb took the punishment that the people deserved for the bad things they had done.

In the middle of all this preparation, Jesus turned to two of His closest friends, Peter and John. He had an important job for them. "Go and get everything ready for our Passover meal," He told them. They knew this meant preparing the lamb for everyone to eat. Eating lamb was a big part of the Passover celebration. Many people enjoyed its taste. In fact, it was considered quite a treat. Even centuries later, when church leaders went out to eat, they would often choose lamb if someone else was paying for the meal.

But the lamb at this Passover was more than just tasty food. It connected the people to their history, reminding them of how God had saved their ancestors from slavery in Egypt. On this particular night, with Jesus at the table, the lamb was about to take on an even deeper meaning. As Peter and John headed off to make the preparations, they had no idea that this Passover meal would be the start of something that would change the world forever.

The First Upper Room

Jesus gave Peter and John very specific instructions. He told them what to look for when they entered the city. "Keep your eyes open," He said. "You'll see a man carrying a jar of water. That's not something you see every day, is it? Usually, it's the women who carry water." (I'm paraphrasing His words in this retelling.) This unusual sight would be their signal. "Follow that man," Jesus continued, "and he'll lead you to the right house."

It was like a secret mission. The disciples were to go up to the owner of the house and say something that sounded like a code: "The Teacher wants to know where the guest room is. He needs a place to eat the Passover meal with His disciples."

Jesus assured them that the owner would understand. He would take them upstairs to show them a large room, all set up and ready for a group. "It won't be a tiny, cramped space," Jesus emphasized. "It will be a big room, with plenty of space for all of us."

Can you picture it? A large room on the upper level, maybe with windows looking out over the city. It would be the place perfect for Jesus and His friends to share this important meal.

Peter and John must have been excited and a bit nervous as they set off. Would everything happen just as Jesus had said? To their amazement, it did! They found the man with the water jar, followed him, and discovered the room exactly as Jesus had described it.

The two disciples couldn't help but be impressed. How did Jesus know all this? It was another reminder that their Teacher was no ordinary man. As they began to prepare the Passover meal in that large upstairs room, they probably wondered what other surprises the evening might bring.

The Continuity of Luke's Gospel and Acts

Now, before we go further, let's talk about the person who wrote down this amazing story. There's a consensus among many mainline biblical scholars that a man named Luke wrote both the Gospel of Luke and the book of Acts. There is continuity between them, as if he wrote a two-part story about Jesus and what happened after Jesus went back to heaven.

The Luke who wrote the gospel book is traditionally considered to be the same person who wrote the book of Acts. Both books are addressed to a person named Theophilus and have similar writing styles and themes. Early Christian tradition attributes both works to Luke, a physician by profession and a companion of the apostle Paul. This attribution is supported by the fact that the author of Acts often uses the first-person plural, *we*, when describing Paul's journeys, suggesting that he was a close companion of Paul.

Remember how we talked about Peter and John following the man with the water jar to find the large upper-level room? Well, Luke didn't stop his story there. He continued it in the book of Acts, picking up right where he left off in his gospel book. In Acts, Luke tells us more about what happened in that upper room (quite likely the same place in each book), and the amazing things that came after. It's as if he is saying, "But wait, there's more!" He shows us how the small group of Jesus' followers in that room grew into a movement that spread across the whole world.

By understanding that Luke most likely wrote both books, we can see the bigger picture. It's not just about one meal in one room. It's the beginning of a story that keeps going, showing how Jesus' life and teachings changed everything.

So, as we read about Peter and John preparing the Passover meal, we're not just hearing about one event. We're seeing the start of something huge that Luke wanted everyone to know about. The first upper-room experience is like a domino that drops and causes a ripple effect of dominos falling as each event unfolds. God has a very unique place in history's unfolding for you too. Even as you're reading this, I've already prayed that the Holy Spirit would allow you to see a generational domino dropping—you're next! Luke carefully wrote it all down from the beginning so that people like you and me, even today, could understand what happened and why we matter in the greater story.

The first upper-room experience is like a domino that drops and causes a ripple effect of dominos falling as each event unfolds. God has a very unique place in history's unfolding for you too.

Let's continue building on what we've learned so far. Long ago, God made a special agreement with His people. We call this the "Old Covenant." It was like a promise between God and humanity, sealed with the blood of a lamb. Every year during

Passover, people would bring an unblemished lamb to the temple to be sacrificed, asking God to forgive their mistakes. The priests would collect the blood and sprinkle it on the altar, symbolizing atonement for the people's sins. Then the lamb would be taken home and roasted, and families would partake of the Passover meal, eating the meat along with unleavened bread and bitter herbs. It would have been a big celebration, complete with live music and palpable joy! The people's sins were forgiven and temporarily atoned for!

But God had an even better plan in mind, a "New Covenant." Instead of having the people sacrifice lambs over and over, God sent Jesus. Now, Jesus wasn't actually a lamb, but He was like one in a special way. Called the Lamb of God, He came to take the place of all those sacrificial lambs, once and for all.

Remember that large upper room where Peter and John prepared the Passover meal? Well, that room saw some incredible things! First, Jesus shared His last meal there with His friends. Then, after Jesus died on the cross and came back to life, He met with His followers again, probably in that same upper room (although we can't prove it).

Luke, our careful writer, tells us what happened next. Jesus told His friends to stay in Jerusalem and wait for a special gift from God—the Holy Spirit. He told them, "John baptized people with water, but soon you'll be baptized with the Holy Spirit" (see Acts 1:5). It was as if Jesus was saying, *Something amazing is about to happen!*

And, did it ever! On a day called Pentecost, when Jesus' followers were all together, something incredible occurred. Suddenly, they heard a sound like a strong wind blowing through the whole house (see Acts 2:1–4). It was the beginning of something big!

This was the start of the New Covenant in action. Instead of a lamb being sacrificed in the temple, Jesus had offered Himself once and for all. Now God's Spirit was coming to live inside people, changing them from the inside out. This is salvation, and this is what it means to be baptized with the Holy Spirit.

Luke shows us how everything is connected: the Passover meal, Jesus' death and resurrection, and this amazing moment when the Holy Spirit arrived not just on earth, but to live inside us as believers. It's one big story, showing how God set up a cascading effect of one event, like a domino, dropping onto another event. The cause-and-effect relationship is what caused a group of early believers to turn into a global movement spanning two thousand years by the time of this writing! Revival is your inheritance.

Not Just Ordinary Fire

Remember how the Passover lamb was roasted in fire? This wasn't just about cooking the meat. The fire was part of the process, the final step in preparing the sacrifice. For centuries, Jewish families had seen this as a sacred act. Fast-forward to that upper room on the day of Pentecost. Something extraordinary happened that would have caught the attention of anyone familiar with the Passover traditions. Just as the lamb was finished by fire, God's Spirit came with what looked like tongues of fire upon each person!

Imagine the scene: The disciples were waiting, just as Jesus had told them to. Suddenly, the rush of wind filled the room, and then came the fire. But this wasn't ordinary fire. It separated into individual flames, one resting on each person there. It was as if God was saying, *The old way is complete. Now I'm doing something new!*

This wasn't just any fire. It was God's presence, coming to live inside each believer. Just as the fire of the altar completed the sacrifice, this holy fire marked the completion of Jesus' work. The disciples were being transformed, like the Passover lamb, but for a new purpose. Then something else amazing happened. They started speaking in languages they had never learned! It was as if the fire had lit up their tongues. They weren't just talking; they were praising God in ways everyone who heard it could understand, no matter where they came from.

People outside heard the commotion and came running. They were amazed to hear their own languages being spoken by these Galileans. Some were so confused by it that they thought the disciples must be drunk! That's when Peter stood up. Remember Peter? He was one of the two who had prepared the Passover meal in (likely) that very room not long ago. Now, filled with the Holy Spirit, he began to explain what was happening. "These people aren't drunk," he said (see Acts 2:14–47). "God is doing something new, just as He promised long ago!"

Peter's words were powerful. They cut straight to people's hearts. By the end of the day, about three thousand people had decided to follow Jesus. The Church was born, and it was growing fast! This was more than just an exciting event. It was the start of a new era. The fire that had once roasted the Passover lamb now burned in the hearts of believers. The sacrifice was complete, and God's Spirit was empowering people to spread the Good News of the gospel all over the world.

Twenty-Four True New Covenant Signs

From that upper room, a movement began that would change history. The story that had started with a simple Passover meal became a worldwide celebration of God's redemption of us and our adoption. When we read the book of Acts, we see the original template for how we ought to live our lives and function as believers. Luke recorded a time that represents the purity of the Church. As you take a deeper look into the stories that unfold in his retelling, very clear signs of what it means to be a true New Covenant believer emerge. Luke gives us twenty-four signs that the Holy Spirit, dwelling inside believers, is active and moving without restraint. This is how we exist when we commit to "stay wild," untamed by false religion and man-made ideologies.

Twenty-Four Signs of a True New Covenant Church

1. *All the believers were coming together in one place.*
   Regular communal worship is essential, as believers come together in one place to share in fellowship and spiritual growth.

2. *There are sounds from heaven.*
   This refers to supernatural manifestations of God's presence, which may include audible phenomena like shouting, celebrating, groaning and travailing in prayer, and speaking in tongues. Sounds can also mean melodies and songs containing prophetic declarations or proclamations of the gospel.

3. *Those baptized in the Spirit each had a tongue of fire above their heads.*
   The Church should witness and experience tangible demonstrations of the Holy Spirit's work among its members. All believers, not just a few leaders, should operate in the gifts of the Spirit. Additionally, the "tongues of fire" were above each head on the day of

Pentecost, which means that in the upper room they couldn't see their own flame, but rather the flames of others. It wasn't represented in their hands, but over their heads. I believe this could be God's way of saying that we must recognize each other's flames instead of obsessing over our own.

4. *People still on the outside will be amazed and astonished.*

   The Church's activities and the move of the Spirit should be noteworthy enough to capture attention and provoke wonder even in unsaved people.

5. *The gospel will be declared.*

   All believers should be empowered to share their faith openly and without fear.

6. *Believers will appear drunk (in the Spirit).*

   This refers to being so filled with the Spirit that one's behavior may appear unusual or ecstatic to outside observers. This includes supernatural boldness! (I myself am an introvert by nature yet have received this boldness.)

7. *Sons and daughters will prophesy.*

8. *Young men will see visions.*

9. *Old men will dream dreams.*

10. *Men and women will prophesy.*

11. *There will be wonders in the heavens and signs in the earth below.*

    This refers to observable cosmic phenomena that point to the sovereignty of God and His divine control (see Matthew 24:29). In other words, a New Testament Church will increase in its discernment concerning warnings or heralds of what is to come.

12. *There will be preaching that cuts to the heart.*

13. *There will be repentance and baptism.*

14. *Thousands will be added.*
This indicates exponential, instantaneous growth as a result of large, historic gatherings such as the Times Square event I did where thousands gathered and said yes to Christ.

15. *There will be devotion to sound teaching.*

16. *Fellowship will be vital.*

17. *Eating together will happen often.*

18. *Signs and wonders will take place.*
These are miraculous events that demonstrate God's power and confirm the truth of the gospel message. Such events will involve believers functioning in delegated authority not only to preach the gospel, but to have signs and wonders occasionally accompanying their proclamation of its message.

19. *Those in the Church will share all things in common.*
Believers are not being territorial or selfish, but are willing to share their resources with each other.

20. *Day by day, believers will attend the temple (local church) and breaking bread in homes.*
Regular attendance at both large gatherings and home meetings is a priority, with a balance between corporate worship and smaller, more intimate group settings.

21. *Gladness will be evident among the believers, as well as generous hearts.*
An atmosphere of joy is evident, along with a willingness to give freely to the mission of the Church and to others.

22. *Believers will always be praising God.*
    Believers exhibit an attitude of worship that permeates
    all aspects of their lives, not just formal church services.
23. *Believers will have favor with people.*
    This includes addressing the needs of the community
    and advocating for justice and righteousness in society.
24. *The Church will add to its numbers daily.*
    This is reflected in incremental increase over time
    through consistent, faithful gospel proclamation, and
    discipleship (what you see after the Acts 2 exponential
    growth moment).

From that explosive day of Pentecost, the early Church began
to grow and spread. What happened in that upper room wasn't
just a one-time event; it was the beginning of a new way of
living for believers. The story that started with Jesus sharing
the Passover meal and continued through His death and resurrection now took on a new chapter with the outpouring of
the Holy Spirit. Living with an expectancy and awareness of
Christ's imminent return, believers were motivated to holy living and an urgent carrying out of their mission to spread the
Good News of the gospel.

When we look closely at Acts chapter 2, we see that Pentecost wasn't just about speaking in tongues. It was a complete
package—all twenty-four signs of God's presence and power
were on display in just this second chapter! This was the full
experience of the New Covenant that Jesus had promised.
Now, here's where it gets really exciting for us today: Many
of us have thought of revival as something special, something
that happens once in a while when God moves in a powerful
way. But when we truly understand what the New Covenant

means, we realize that we should be living in a state of constant revival!

Speaking in tongues, which we saw happen at Pentecost, is a big part of this. It's called *glossolalia* in scientific terms, but really, it's a special gift from God that allows believers to pray and worship in a language they haven't learned. Some people think this gift was only for the early Church and that it stopped being available after those first Christians. But that's not what the Bible teaches us. In fact, the Bible makes it clear that speaking in tongues is a gift from God meant for all believers, even today. It's not just a historical event; it's a current reality that can transform our prayer lives and our connection with God.

But remember, it's not just about tongues. It's about embracing all aspects of Pentecost: the power, the boldness, the unity, and the miracles. When we open ourselves up to the full experience of the Holy Spirit, just like those first believers in the upper room, we position ourselves for sustained revival.

Imagine what our churches, our families, and our world would look like if we lived every day in the full power of Pentecost. This isn't just a dream; it's the reality that God intended for His Church.

By understanding and embracing the fullness of the New Covenant, including gifts like speaking in tongues, we can step into a life of continuous, transformative revival. So let's not settle for occasional spiritual highs. Let's dive deep into the meaning of Pentecost, explore all the gifts God has for us, and live in the sustained revival that Jesus made possible through His sacrifice and through sending the Holy Spirit. This is the exciting journey of faith that the early Church began, and it's the journey we are invited to continue today!

Tongues and Revival Today

Who can speak in tongues? And why is this important for revival? In Mark 16:17, Jesus says that signs will follow the ones who believe: "And these signs will accompany those who believe: in my name they will cast out demons; they will speak in new tongues." He didn't say these signs would only follow pastors, self-proclaimed apostles, Pentecostals, or charismatics. He said *those who believe*. If you believe that Jesus is the Messiah and you follow Him, then these signs will follow *you*.

One of the biggest attacks of the enemy across generations has been to silence the gift of tongues. When you read about mighty moves of God historically, you'll see a constant thread is prayer and intercession. The first-century Church understood the importance of praying in the Spirit, and every awakening, renewal, and revival is a restoration of this revelation.

As a Fire Starter, you must resolve never to be persuaded by doctrines of demons masquerading as intellectualism. You are being equipped to understand the truth of the Scriptures. Under the Old Covenant, humankind interacted with God through a mediator. Receiving forgiveness required sacrificial systems, which involved the bloodshed of animals. A high priest would go into the Holy of Holies, where the presence of God dwelt, on the people's behalf. God takes covenants very seriously. An existing covenant can only be ended by the establishment of a new one. When Jesus died and was resurrected on the third day, He began the New Covenant. He promised that He would baptize the disciples with the Holy Spirit:

> On one occasion, while he was eating with them, he gave them this command: "Do not leave Jerusalem, but wait for the gift my Father promised, which you have heard me speak about. For John baptized with water, but in a few days you will be baptized with the Holy Spirit."
>
> Acts 1:4–5 NIV

In Acts 2:1–4, the disciples were all in one place and in one accord, and Jesus inaugurated the New Covenant by giving them the gift of tongues, as we learned earlier:

> When the day of Pentecost arrived, they were all together in one place. And suddenly there came from heaven a sound like a mighty rushing wind, and it filled the entire house where they were sitting. And divided tongues as of fire appeared to them and rested on each one of them. And they were all filled with the Holy Spirit and began to speak in other tongues as the Spirit gave them utterance.

What Jesus established by His sacrifice is forever—it's not going to change. Anything that the finished work of the cross put in place is still in place today. There will not be a third covenant. Some say that the gift of tongues ceased with the early Church. Yet in order for that to be true, another covenant would have had to be enacted to replace the one established at the cross. Because again, the only way to end a covenant is to establish a newer covenant. That's not going to happen, because Jesus isn't going to die again. His death and resurrection are a finished work. The gift of tongues is active and has not ceased, and the proof is that the New Covenant is still in operation.

The Gift of Tongues Is Free

The gift of speaking in tongues is called a gift because it's free. It carried a high price that you and I could never pay for with our own good works. Jesus Himself paid for it with His life, and all we have to do is ask for it.

It's a gift, it's for you, and it's for now. It's that simple. In all of my years ministering, I've noticed a pattern among those who struggle to receive the gift. They tend to be very hard to give any gift to. They are often hard workers, independent, and the kind of people who take care of others. When God extends the gift of speaking in tongues, they struggle to receive it because it's much more logical for them to earn it. They are trapped in a paradigm of "works."

But notice, we don't call what God has for us "the rewards of the Spirit," but rather "the gifts of the Spirit." Rewards are earned, but gifts are received. Revival is not a reward; it's an inheritance. This is why you often see a correlation between large numbers of people receiving the gift of tongues and a simultaneous explosion of revival. The common thread is learning to receive instead of to achieve. When full surrender occurs in the life of a believer, it doesn't just mean giving things up; it also means understanding the revelation of adoption as a son or daughter of the King, and being able to accept all that He is extending.

Even as I write this, I can sense the Holy Spirit drawing you nearer and nearer. At any point, you can say, *Holy Spirit, I'm ready to receive the gifts You have for me.* At the age of fifteen, despite crippling social anxiety, introversion, and trauma from my past, I said those words and had a personal Pentecost. Right on the edge of my bed, I was baptized by the Holy Spirit and received my heavenly language!

Four Types of Tongues

Let's go to 1 Corinthians 14:2: "For one who speaks in a tongue speaks not to men but to God." When you read that, you might think, *Wait a second, though—already it seems as if the Bible is contradicting itself. What about Acts 2, where the first time tongues showed up, everybody within earshot understood them?*

That's a fair question, so let's take a closer look at this seeming contradiction. Write 1 Corinthians 14:2 down in your notes first (the whole verse this time): "For one who speaks in a tongue speaks not to men but to God; for no one understands him, but he utters mysteries in the Spirit." Then go back and think about Acts 2 again. The first tongues that showed up were actually in other languages that were known to men, and people understood them as they heard the gospel and the wondrous things of God being declared. In one case, no one understands a tongue in which someone is speaking only to God and uttering mysteries in the Spirit. In the other case, everyone understands the tongues being spoken. So again, you might ask, *Isn't the Bible therefore contradicting itself?*

No, it's not. There are *different kinds* of tongues. A lot of the offense and issues people have with tongues in the local church is because they don't have a sound biblical interpretation and understanding of the different kinds of tongues. It is important to differentiate between *public* tongues and *private* tongues, and then also to understand how tongues are to be used publicly.

Now, let's go to 1 Corinthians 14:14, where Paul says, "For if I pray in a tongue . . ." Compare that to Acts 2, where the believers were praying to God in the upper room, but then when the Holy Spirit came upon them, they started proclaiming

174

publicly about the mighty works of God in a different tongue. From this we see that you can pray in one tongue, but then you can proclaim in another tongue.

Actually, there are four types of tongues that we need to understand: *public tongues as signs to unbelievers, public tongues for interpretation, private tongues for intercession,* and *private tongues for personal prayer.* Let's take a moment and look at each of these more closely to make sure that we have a solid biblical understanding of them.

1. Public tongues as signs to unbelievers

This type of tongue is more proclamation than prayer, and it's a sign to unbelievers. We see it first in Acts 2. I do believe that it's possible for you to go overseas or go into various other environments and speak in tongues that people around you would understand, and this would be a sign to any unbelievers. In other words, they would hear your proclamation in a language that they know you don't know, and they would understand you, which actually becomes a sign to them.

As 1 Corinthians 14:22 says, "Thus tongues are a sign not for believers but for unbelievers, while prophecy is a sign not for unbelievers but for believers." This could be a seeming contradiction, which we also need to unpack a little bit. It just means that there are different types of prophecy, and there are different types of tongues. We must go back to what the apostle Paul was talking about in order to say what kind of prophecy and what kind of tongues. Does this make sense? It does clarify the issue.

One time I was interceding for my sister, and what I was speaking sounded as if it was Italian. I wrote it down phonetically and brought it back to my Italian professor at Indiana University. She asked, "Where did you get this?"

I answered, "I'm not going to tell you. You tell me what it means."

Then she said, "This is an older, archaic version of Italian, and it looks as though you're saying, 'Sarah, I will wash you clean; Sarah, I will make you pure.'"

My sister's name is Sarah.

2. Public tongues for interpretation

This is the tongue that Paul talks about in 1 Corinthians 14:27: "If any speak in a tongue, let there be only two or three at most, and each in turn, and let someone interpret." This type of tongue may be heard spoken aloud during a church service or a group gathering, where someone speaks a prophetic word in a language unknown to him or her, and another person is given the gift of interpreting its meaning for the congregation. Paul instructs that this should be done in an orderly way, to ensure the understanding and edification of all present (see 1 Corinthians 14:26–33). When the Holy Spirit moves in this way, one speaker voices utterances in an unknown language and another believer translates the message, thereby benefitting the entire assembly. This demonstrates how the Spirit works through different members of the Body of Christ to communicate His truth.

3. Private tongues for intercession

Romans 8:26 gives us an example of this tongue: "Likewise the Spirit helps us in our weakness. For we do not know what to pray for as we ought, but the Spirit himself intercedes for us with groanings too deep for words." This is a form of prayer where the Holy Spirit helps us pray when we don't know what to pray for. While these groanings are described as being "too deep for words" in our natural understanding, they may be expressed through speaking in tongues—utterances in languages not native to us. In these intimate moments of prayer, the Holy Spirit can move through both wordless groanings and supernatural languages, giving voice to deep spiritual yearnings that our natural words cannot adequately express.

4. Private tongues for personal prayer

This is a kind of tongues just for your own building up. It's for strengthening you. For an example of this one, we can return to 1 Corinthians 14:2: "For one who speaks in a tongue speaks not to men but to God; for no one understands him, but he utters mysteries in the Spirit."

John Bevere shared an illuminating parallel that helps us understand the power of unknown languages. During World War II, we were losing against the Japanese because they were able to decipher our codes and our language very easily. There was a former missionary who had learned a Native American language, however, which had not necessarily been completely recorded. He came to the United States military and taught them this language, and the Japanese were unable to break that code. That actually became the impetus for us to start taking ground to win that battle. While this example involves a human language rather than a spiritual tongue, I believe it illustrates how the Holy Spirit's wisdom can work through languages unknown to our adversary. Speaking in tongues and uttering mysteries in the Spirit becomes a language that cannot be penetrated by demonic monitoring spirits that want to come in and gather intel on the strategy of God. There's a statement "loose lips sink ships." Sometimes, you need to stop speaking English (or whatever your native language is) in your prayer time, because the devil is discerning the situation and possibly breaking the code of what God might do. Remember that although the devil is not omniscient and does not know the future, he does know the character, nature, and attributes of God. Sometimes, speaking in tongues becomes a form of warfare that says to the devil, *Try to crack this code, homey.*

Addressing Cessationism

I've spent much time talking about theology in many circles, and I love cessationists. I have friends who are cessationists, and we have great and wonderful conversations about the Scriptures together. I'm not dogging those types of people, nor dissing them. But what I've noticed about them, if I am able to make a fair generalization, is that they tend to view the things that are emotional as immature, and they tend to believe that the things we Pentecostals say are spiritual are actually emotional.

I believe that if we are going to experience the fullness of freedom, of course there will be things we do that are emotional— but emotion is not always immaturity. You have to disconnect the word *immature* from the word *emotional.* You also cannot make the mistake of thinking that being stoic is the same as being mature.

You likewise have to disconnect from the idea that just because you don't know big words, you are not intelligent. There are people who memorize big words but still have average IQs. This is why other theologians listen to me teach; they know I know the terminologies, but they also know I'm not trying to impress people with my knowledge. I'm trying to transmit God's knowledge, and if you don't understand it, I have failed. The goal is not to wow you with words; it is to transform you with God's Word.

Often, cessationists and others will try to say that the gift of tongues is not for today. They will look at our displays of worship and at the way we do church, and dismiss it as immaturity or a theologically low IQ. I would submit to them the idea that whom the Son sets free is free indeed, and I'm free to worship with full expression. I'm free to speak in tongues. I'm free. Why? Because my mind doesn't benefit from it, but my spirit does. For a number of people in the cessationist camp, their struggle involves the pride of life, which is intellectualism, which is in the realm of the mind. They claim that we function in the realm of our emotions, but the mind and the emotions are both faculties of the soul.

I'm not saying that we do things out of the soulless realm; rather, we do them out of the spirit realm. Oftentimes when prayer and worship flow from the spirit, this will also activate realms of the soul, which are your mind *and* your emotions.

As a matter of fact, I would say to some of those who don't see the gifts as for today, the most profitable thing for you would be a demonstration of your emotions, because whom the Son sets free is free indeed. This means that yes, you can intellectually prosper, you can prosper in your soul, but you can also prosper in your spirit. What if it was "all of your being" engaged in worship and devotion?

A Story of Perpetual Revival

As the sun sets on Jerusalem, casting long shadows across the ancient stones, we find ourselves back in that upper room where it all began. The air is thick with anticipation, echoing the very breath of God that first stirred over the waters of creation. This is where the old gives way to the new, where the story of redemption takes an unexpected turn.

Remember the Passover lamb, roasted by fire, with its blood as a symbol of salvation? Now, in this very room, tongues of fire dance above the heads of believers, marking them as living sacrifices. The sacrifice is no longer on an altar of stone, but in the hearts of men and women set ablaze by the Holy Spirit.

From this sacred space, a revolution of love spreads like wildfire. The disciples, once cowering in fear, now boldly proclaim the Good News in languages they never learned. It's as if Babel's curse is being undone, unity emerging from diversity. This is Pentecost—not just a historical event, but a perpetual invitation to revival.

How do we step into this river of living water? It begins with forgiveness. As we release the burdens of bitterness and hurt, we create space for the Holy Spirit to flood our beings. Our tongues, once instruments of cursing, become conduits of heavenly mysteries. We speak not by force, but by faith, allowing the Spirit to empower us, just as He empowers us to witness.

This gift of tongues is not just about speaking unknown languages; it's about breaking down barriers between heaven and earth, between God and His children. It's an intimate conversation with the Divine, uttering mysteries too deep for human words. Whether in public proclamation or private prayer, it's a reminder that we are no longer orphans, but sons and daughters of the Most High.

As we learn to host the Holy Spirit—through holiness, overflowing grace, sanctification, and teachability—we create an atmosphere where miracles become commonplace. The twenty-four signs of a true New Covenant Church aren't just a checklist, but a vivid portrait of a community ablaze with God's presence.

From that upper room to your living room, from ancient Jerusalem to the bustling streets of New York City, and all over the world, the same Spirit is moving, calling, and transforming. He is inviting you into a story far grander than you could imagine—a story of perpetual revival, of heaven touching earth.

So, open your heart, let go of unforgiveness, lift your hands, and as you do, feel the gentle breeze of the Spirit stirring within you. It is not forced; it is not coerced. It is a gift freely given, waiting for you to receive it by faith.

This is your moment. This is your Pentecost. As you step out in faith, may your tongue be loosed, may your spirit soar, and may you find yourself swept up in the magnificent, unfolding story of God's redemptive love. The upper-room experience isn't just history; it's your inheritance. Embrace it, live it, and watch as the fire of revival spreads through you to a world desperate for hope.

MIKE SIGNORELLI is a pastor, film director, content creator, YouTuber, author, philanthropist, and speaker. His humble beginnings growing up in impoverished Chicagoland led him to pursue higher education and eventually to answer the call to preach and lead.

Mike is the pastor and founder of V1 Church, a vibrant and growing community of believers around the world. With physical church locations in Long Island, Brooklyn, Manhattan, New Jersey, Miami, and Northwest Indiana, he also has a global church community with hundreds of online watch parties meeting weekly. V1 Church was listed at No. 26 in *Outreach* magazine's "Outreach 100 Fastest-Growing Churches" in America in 2023 and has been called the "fastest-growing church in America" from 2017 to 2021 by INJOY Stewardship Solutions.

Pastor Mike started a teaching broadcast during the COVID-19 pandemic that grew to over five million viewers per month across social platforms. As a result, V1 College was established to provide leadership and theological training, and currently has more than two hundred students enrolled from over twenty nations.

He also developed The Breakers App, which features The Breakers Certification, a course that trains Breakers worldwide in the basics of evangelism, healing, prophecy, and deliverance ministry.

After escaping the poverty of his early years, Mike was motivated to help young families thrive. Seeing many people struggle for basic necessities in New York City Metro, he and his wife, Julie, responded by creating a nonprofit called V1 Community Impact. Consequently, the foundation provides a Christmas miracle to hundreds of people in shelters between Brooklyn and Long Island. In addition, hundreds of families receive food monthly through the foundation's philanthropic work.

Mike is an accomplished author, having self-published several books that have been well-received by audiences around the world. His newest book, *Inherit Your Freedom*, was released by Chosen Books in 2024 and obtained bestseller status. In 2023, Mike wrote and directed the movie *The Domino Revival*, based on his own life story. The film played in over one thousand theaters nationwide, and moviegoers experienced healing, deliverance, and salvation, and some even canceled suicides.

Aside from his work as a content creator, filmmaker, pastor, author, and philanthropist, Mike is also a sought-after speaker who travels the world speaking at church gatherings, conferences, tent revivals, and festivals.

Mike and Julie have two daughters, Everly Faith and Bella Joy. They currently reside in New York City.

OUTRO

MIKE SIGNORELLI

If you've made it to this point, you've already proven that you truly are a Fire Starter. The emotion, the hype, it all wears off—and then the single determining factor of greatness in the Kingdom becomes enduring until the end. What all great men and women have in common is an unwavering commitment fueled by a deep, immovable conviction that what they are doing is what needs to be done.

We who wrote these pages simply could not know the circumstances or specific conditions that you would encounter in your life and walk, but remember that the problems you face, you were created to solve.

They call it adversity; we call it opportunity.

They call it impossibility; we call it divine inspiration.

They see barriers; we see breakthroughs.

They fear the unknown; we ignite the unseen.

For where others perceive darkness, Fire Starters illuminate a new path to revival.

This book is a baton, and now it has been handed to you. Start a fire.

—Mike Signorelli

NOTES

Chapter 1 Consecration and Revival

1. Larry Pierce, *The Outline of Biblical Usage*, "H6942 - qāḏaš," Blue Letter Bible, https://www.blueletterbible.org/lexicon/h6942/kjv/wlc/0-1/.

2. Frank Bartleman, *How Pentecost Came to Los Angeles: As It Was in the Beginning*, which can be found at https://www.ccel.org/ccel/bartleman /los/formats/los.pdf. The quote is on page 13 of chapter 1.

3. D. Martyn Lloyd-Jones, *Revival* (Crossway Books, 1987), 47.

Chapter 2 The Ripple Effects of Revival

1. Dr. James Strong, "Strong's Definitions," "G3708 - horaō," Blue Letter Bible, https://www.blueletterbible.org/lexicon/g3708/kjv/tr/0-1/.

2. Charles Finney, *Lectures on Revivals of Religion* (Revell, 1868), "Lecture I: What a Revival of Religion Is," found in the Christian Classics Ethereal Library, https://ccel.org/ccel/finney/revivals/revivals.iii.i.html.

Chapter 4 The Zeal of the Lord

1. Bill Mounce, Greek Dictionary, "Strong's G2205 - zēlos," For an Informed Love of God website, https://www.billmounce.com/greek-dictionary /zelos.

Chapter 5 Revival and Evangelism: The Divine Partnership

1. "Churchgoers Believe in Sharing Faith, Most Never Do," *Lifeway Research*, August 13, 2012, https://research.lifeway.com/2012/08/13/churchgoers -believe-in-sharing-faith-most-never-do/.

2. Thabiti Anyabwile, "105 People Die Each Minute," TGC (The Gospel Coalition), October 24, 2016, https://www.thegospelcoalition.org/article/105 -people-die-each-minute/.

Chapter 7 Surrender

1. I've related to you my version of this story, but you can read the original version here: Reinhard Bonnke, "Parable: Victorious Living," *Christ for All Nations*, https://cfan.org.uk/connect/bible-studies/parable-victorious-living.

2. Jentezen Franklin, *The Amazing Discernment of Women: Learning to Understand Your Spiritual Intuition and God's Plan for It* (Thomas Nelson, 2006), 29.

3. *The Letters of John Wesley*, letter to George Cussons, London, November 18, 1768, found as #31 at the Wesley Center Online, https://wesley.nnu.edu/john-wesley/the-letters-of-john-wesley/wesleys-letters-1768.

4. Don Whitney, *Spiritual Disciplines for the Christian Life* (NavPress, 1991), 166.

Chapter 9 The Coming Family Revival

1. To hear Dutch Sheets talk more about this, visit King of Kings Worship Center, "Dutch Sheets: Ecclesia NOW! Operating in Two Spheres of Authority (Ephesians 4:11–12)," run time 22:43, Facebook, September 29, 2020, https://www.facebook.com/kingofkingswc/videos/794779204659330/.

2. For more on the Greek word *apocalypto*, see the Blue Letter Bible entry for apokalyptō, found at https://www.blueletterbible.org/lexicon/g601/esv/mgnt/0-1/.

www.ingramcontent.com/pod-product-compliance
Lightning Source LLC
Chambersburg PA
CBHW030250100426
42812CB00002B/386